Paul...

I'M UGLY AND BROKE
IT AIN'T BAD WHEN YOU GET USED TO IT!

KENNESAW TAYLOR
MILLEDGEVILLE, GA

WWW.KENNESAWTAYLOR.COM

phillip think you for all
your support. R hope you like
this
Kennesaw

LEMON PRESS

ISBN: 978-0-9844183-8-1

CONTENTS

INTRODUCTION

I'm Ugly and Broke
It Ain't Bad When You Get Used To It!

I greet everyone I meet with these words. It's a joke to me, but you should see the looks I get from others. The regular people laugh at it, the ones with a little too much starch in their shorts step back and make some idiotic comment about not wanting to be near that much negativity. Get over yourself; life is supposed to be fun. This is a good way to pick who'll be sitting with you at dinner. If you don't get the title you are probably about as much fun at a party as the grim reaper.

This book is filled with my columns, the funny and the serious ones. It's got a few poems, the funny ones and the Icky sicky ones. It's got some of my stuff that wouldn't get into the papers; yeah I write such stuff too. It's got a few short stories; I tend to be a little dark with those. I guess it's got all the stuff I've written over the last year, both fit and not fit for print.

You must remember that everything that comes from the mind of man isn't fit for the newspapers, so here you get a little taste of what won't make it to the news stand. I hope this doesn't start too much crap, or maybe I hope it does. I am what I am and I write what is given me. I've had a great year, wrote a lot and prepared several books to go to print. I've been traveling all over Georgia speaking and doing book signings. Thanks to all of you that have made this the best year of my life. Look me up on facebook or just drop me a line at kennesawt@gmail.com. The book Informally Educated has been selling a lot better than the big publishers would admit. If you haven't read it yet please give it a try. I'm just a country boy who has something to say and it seems a few are listening.

KennesawTaylor

CRITTERS

Road Kill Bill

I'm pretty sure none of you know my friend Bill Shirley, if you do, please don't let him know I told you this story. A few years back, he took a trip to the mountains to visit family. While he was there he decided to find out if White County moonshine was any better than its Wilkinson County counterpart, he assures me it's not. Now it could be argued that if he was a smart man he'd not have tried it in the first place. It could be further argued that he'd never have gotten in a car afterward; no matter how small an amount he tried. I'm not about to argue with you, truth is, old Bill just ain't that smart.

Having said that, that's exactly what he did. Driving down the interstate headed home, only slightly buzzed, he noticed a dead, bear cub lying on the side of the road. It took him all of two exits to convince himself that there'd never be another chance for a boy from Wilkinson County to get a bear skin to put in his den. He turned around and headed back. After all it was just a big ball of fur.

Looking carefully in his mirrors while the sun was setting, he pulled over and quickly threw the 100 pound bear in the back seat to share the ride with the 2 gallons of White County's finest already making the trip. Somewhere in or around Gainesville, the bear proved to have only been knocked out. Bill tells me and I believe him, that the last thing you want to do is find yourself in a car with two gallons of whiskey and a mad 100 pound bear.

That little ball of fur proceeded to rip the back seat apart. Almost instantly it destroyed one or both of the jugs, the smell in the car became so strong Bill could hardly see. Add to this that Bill was trying to get stopped, hoping the bear didn't notice there was a front seat and much less, he was in it. As soon as the car slowed down enough Bill bailed out, trapping the cub inside. The car ran into the median and stopped on a culvert.

Bill says, and again I believe him, "You really got to reevaluate your life when you're a boy from Wilkinson County, standing in Hall County, with a White County bear and 2 gallons of illegal whiskey in your back seat."

He had no idea what to do. The bear was so mad he was afraid to open the door and let it out. He didn't have to worry about it long. A State Trooper showed up shortly. It took 5 Troopers, 2 Hall County deputies and a Game Warden, 2 hours to get the bear out of the car safely, without hurting themselves or it.

Now if Bill was a lucky man, I'm afraid he's no luckier than he is smart, they would've had a good laugh and sent him on his way. He'd have to replace everything inside his car, but what a story he'd have to tell. Turns out, no one present had a sense of humor at all. His weekend visit turned into a 2 week, all expense paid vacation in the Hall County jail. The State kept his car and he ended up paying about 2 grand in fines before Hall County would invite him to never come back again.

Although I know you'd never do something like this, I've just got to give you a little advice here. If you're gonna pick up road kill, for heaven's sake don't let it be an alligator, snake or a bear. If you don't hear that, hear this. If you're gonna pick up road kill, at least check it for a pulse.

The Bear in the Bush

Bob and Anne live in the north Georgia and are friends of mine. They've recently had gastric bypass and trimmed down from their former weights of over four hundred pounds apiece. This story took place before that happened.

It's funny, people who live in middle Georgia want to live in the mountains. People who live in the mountains want to live in the mountains of North Carolina. With this in mind they bought a place to retire, just over the mountain in North Carolina. It's a beautiful little cabin, but is inaccessible during the winter due to elevation and snow. Having bought it in the fall, they endured the longest winter of their lives to wait until they could spend the first weekend there.

This is when we met, I was a car salesman and they bought a new S.U.V from me. Their next stop was to fill the car with as many stores as possible, to stock the cabin. They left Gainesville early on a Saturday morning, to arrive at their new little piece of paradise at nine Am. The drive was amazing, spring was springing.

Pulling up in front of the cabin, they were ecstatic and getting out they opened the rear hatch and carried as many groceries as possible, inside. Piling them on the table, they went out for more. As they stepped onto the porch, a mountain Laurel in full bloom across the yard in the edge of the woods caught their attention and having all the time in the world they moved across to get a better look.

Now this should be a really cute story and I guess it has been so far, but life is not all cute stories. The yard dropped off steeply and they had to be careful as they moved down the bank to get a closer look. By the time they reached the bush, their heads were just barely level with the yard. A noise grabbed their attention and they were horrified to look back and see a large Black Bear, standing upright and entering the cabin door.

They could have just yelled, maybe threw something and ran him off. I've learned with my knees being bad, you don't put yourself in a position to run unless you have too, I think with both of them being so overweight, they had learned that too. Deciding to wait the bear out, they lay on the bank with only the tops of their heads showing. The Bear had found a new party spot. He started ransacking the cabin, breaking windows from the inside out and having a little picnic with the food already taken inside. By the time he came out several hours later, the cabin was in shambles.

He sat down on the front porch and enjoyed the large bag of double stuffed Oreo's they'd just bought, right in front of them. Realize the front yards in the mountains are very small and only twenty feet separated them from the bear. It was at the end of the Oreo's that he discovered the S.U.V sitting there with the hatch open and loaded with all manner of new and exciting foods for him to try.

They watched in horror as he climbed in and started throwing things out. He made the long trip over the seats to the front, got trapped and started freaking out. Somehow in all the pandemonium he started the S.U.V. He did eventually figure out how to get back to where the food was, but only after rearranging the interior of the car. Once in the rear again, he threw their clothing and the rest of the food out into the yard.

They lay on the bank as the sun went down in the night air which was still cold. The bear continued to eat, making several trips back and forth to the cabin. It was daybreak before the bear tired of this and left on his own accord.

The car had run out of gas, they couldn't find their cell phone, seemed the bear needed it worse than they did. The next three days were spent trying to survive on the canned food the bear couldn't open. They had terrible colds and were very stiff from their night exposed to the elements. Eventually someone at the local country store got worried and came looking for them. Thank God for people who don't mind their own business. The car couldn't be driven and had two thousand dollars worth of damage. The cabin cost several thousand to repair also. It was during that night they decided to have bypass surgery, a decision well made.

Over the next year they played cat and mouse with the bear, with some satisfaction as the bear jockeyed to get them into the same situation again. I'm happy to report that he never did and he eventually moved on.

Set my Doggies Free

Most of my story ideas come to me as I walk my dogs, this one happened to me while I was doing that. We were at the beach in 2007 for our anniversary. I'd love to say which one, but the statute of limitations hasn't run out yet. We had a great week, visiting plenty of museums, going to the beach and we were staying in a campground at the beach. As always I got up one morning at 6 am and rather than wake my poor wife at such an ungodly hour, I decided to treat my dogs with a long walk.

So, armed with a large cup of coffee and plenty of cigarettes, I headed down the street. It was a lovely neighborhood with old southern style homes on one side of the street and the beach on the other, the view was amazing. I was enjoying myself very much and the dogs, well they love to walk. After about two miles I decided to get a local newspaper from a box that was just sitting there, looking out of place in this beautiful part of town.

I had picked up my wallet and my change from the table as I left, but had just the right change for a Sunday paper. This day was going great. I hadn't seen a soul and felt relaxed and peaceful. I placed the still half full cup of coffee on top of the machine and dropped the change in the box. Getting out a paper while holding two dog leashes isn't the easiest thing in the world, so the door slipped out of my hands and slammed shut.

My coffee spilled all over me, my dogs, the paper box and the paper I'd just bought. What was more disturbing was that my hand was on one side of the box and the dogs were on the other side with the leashes trapped in the middle by the door. I stepped back and the dogs just stood there on about one foot of leash blinking at me, looking confused. Searching my pockets and my wallet I realized I was stuck bad. I don't know if God was testing me or if the Devil had placed that paper box there just to ruin an otherwise perfect day. I may have said a few choice words to the box, failing some sort of test or other, but I was a little upset. The box, for its part, just stood there and mocked me. I'd like to say it said something to really make me mad, yes I think it did.

I looked in both directions, but no one was in sight, I had no idea what to do. I couldn't leave the dogs there and walk 2 miles back to the camper, there were no businesses nearby. I started up the street, cursing all the while looking for a makeshift key to the paper box. I'm not proud of my decision, but it was the only idea I could come up with and besides that paper box had messed with the wrong man's dogs. About 2 blocks away I found a lawn mower blade in the ditch in front of a vacant lot. Gentlemen choose your weapons. The dogs had no clue what I was doing with it when they watched me return and prepare to do battle with the villainous, paper box. They never barked or even got upset, but sat down with their heads very near the door and looked up at me perplexed. I had a sword fight with this monster and made so much noise in this early morning, perfectly, peacefully neighborhood that I thought I'd wake the whole town up. I cut my hand in the process, but after about 30 minutes of fighting with an inanimate object I won and got the dogs loose.

The paper box sat there in the throws of death, looking sad for the life it had led and all it would never do. I want to believe it was sorry for what it had done to my innocent dogs, but it probably had a hard heart and died with no remorse. I looked up and down the street once more nervously and still no one was in sight. As I turned to make a slow two-mile get away from the scene of the crime, I noticed that the police department was about two blocks away on a side street. My heart started to flutter and I moved off at the fastest pace my heart would allow.

I'm still not proud of what I did that morning, but you just don't mess with my dogs, no matter how important you think you are. Furthermore, it's best not to smart off to an unstable redneck while you're holding his dogs hostage.

KENNESAW TAYLOR

Puppy Dog Toys and Tails

We've discussed my dogs plenty, but for those of you who don't know, I've got two rather large Australian Shepherds living in my house with two cats and two parrots. Well that's not entirely correct. Circumstances moved my mother in with us recently and we could hardly tell her to get rid of her animals. So now we have a Chihuahua, who just happens to think he's a bulldog and two Shiatsus that just, well just think they own the world. Add to this a cat that can't seem to make friends with my two and you've got a pretty chaotic situation.

The cats never really get into it, but it seems they have a mutual destruction thing going on. They growl and hiss at each other all day and every once in a while they go to swinging and chasing each other all over the house. It sounds like they're fighting, but the truth is they're all scared and won't even get close enough to touch. I guess we're lucky they're all cowardly lions.

Our dogs are pretty laid back, so they spend a lot of time just looking at the new arrivals like "Have you lost your mind?" They pay little attention to them and continue to be our children. Our girl dog thinks she's the mother of them all and is very stern, they pretty much know better than to mess with her. The boy will stand there while the Chihuahua attacks him unfazed. He looks like he's smiling as the little fraction of a dog does his worst.

I've always had a kind of sixth sense about getting up in my house in the dark. Anyone breaks in better have it too, because when I get out of bed I know every inch of my house. I can walk through my house, make coffee, get dressed, work at the computer, load my pockets and leave the house with no light whatsoever. The only hold up is that my dogs are black, so I had to learn to drag my feet to keep from stepping on them, not a bad adjustment. Now things have changed and maybe the fact that I'm turning 49 next month has something to do with it. I can't seem to adjust to all the new animals. All the animals have decided that my office is theirs and they look at me like I'm crazy when I try to enter it.

I get up at least two hours before daylight and now there is no place to put a foot without it being on a dog tail, a dog toy or a cat. Dogs and dog toys are similar in the dark to an unsuspecting foot. My dogs usually have two toys. Moms dogs have about 25 and she adds to the number every week or so. I've spilled coffee on most of them, dropped things all over the house, fell down several times and am starting to think I'm going to hurt myself before it's over. The cats stay at odds so they have taken to bad habits. They steal things, hide things and in their rambunctious avoiding of each other, knock over lamps, chairs, boxes and once in a while a person. I've seen cats spinning tires, wipe off an entire counter of papers, keys, nuts, bolt and canisters, scattering it all over the house.

Then what happens if you must walk my mother's dogs? The little black one, the one who's a bulldog in drag, flips and flops like a Mexican jumping bean on steroids the whole time, he pees and poos on the run. He looks like a black balloon on a string with the air running out if it. The other two will not walk on the side of the road, whichever side you're on, they want to be on the other. They will refuse to go out if it looks like rain, smells like rain or even if the dew has fallen. Once in a while they just stop and refuse to start again and when they do, you can count on them being in the middle of the road.

Most of you have been reading my stuff for a while now and I believe that some of you like me. I hope that when you read this you'll have a heart and turn me in to the proper authorities. They'll dispatch a couple guys who'll come down to Ivey, put me in a white jacket and take me for an all expense paid vacation to Milledgeville. If they do, I hope they don't have therapy dogs there.

KENNESAW TAYLOR

Dog Parks and Barks

We were in Savannah for the last 3 days, more specifically on Tybee Island. You must understand we never leave home without our dogs. Our dogs were introduced to a dog park for the first time. River's End campgrounds were just as friendly as they always have been. The addition of two dog parks nearby, by the city of Tybee Island, were a pleasant surprise.

Our dogs got to run and play 3 times a day with all types of dogs and owners. I must tell you we were a little apprehensive about it, since our dogs aren't used to having so much interaction with dogs they don't know. It went great, the other owners were amazing. In the 11 or so visits we met some of the nicest people we've ever met. We met people from all over the country as well as locals. We had amazing conversations, well maybe I did a little too much of the talking, but anyone who knows me isn't surprised.

We were in Savannah for the Hundred Mile bicycle ride Sunday and watched as the riders came in, worn out from a little more wind than they had expected. We met some great people there, including one of my face book friends Norm Lack. Many came in, their bodies stressed and their legs cramping, but not Norm, at sixty he seemed hardly fazed by the ride he'd just completed. It was a pleasure to meet him in person. It's also very nice to meet people and find out they are exactly who they say they are. Norm took copies of the Cracker Jack Crew and Informally Educated back home with him to Hilton Head. I met a navy man who took The Cracker Jack Crew back to his submarine, which is very cool. I really want some sailors to read it.

I put books out at E Shavers a very cool bookstore in the heart of Savannah on Bull Street. Everyone there was extremely nice and I enjoyed the experience. I then stopped at a gelato shop to ask for directions to the Book Lady. She only deals in used books, but was very nice. I returned to Mr. Koolz Gelato Shop on Liberty Street, because my dumb ass didn't even know what one was. I've been all over the world, written four books and had no clue what a gelato was. Janet, the owner, not only sold me one of the best tasting peach treats I've ever eaten, she asked if I would leave some of the books for her to sell. She had a bookshelf on one wall and sells local books. We had a great conversation and I highly recommend to all my dumb ass redneck friends that you find out what a gelato is as soon as possible.

I met Susan at Seaside Sisters, a very cool shop on Tybee Island, who also sells local books, but she said she'd have to read the book before she could put it in her shop. It's the first time that's happened, but I understand. Monday was a day to meet face book friends. Brenda and I met three and signed books for two others who couldn't make it. That was the best part of the weekend. I'll be putting up a few pictures in a few minutes.

On our last visit to the dog park we met a Savannah–Chatham County Police Officer, Brian Krouse, and he took an interest in the book. He got a copy of the Cracker Jack Crew and I look forward to hearing his thoughts.

I came home to a ton of e-mails and a bunch of friend requests on face book from people I didn't even meet. I had a great weekend and met some really good people. I think Informally Educated will explode in Savannah, even more so than it has in the Macon area. I'll be back in Savannah on the 23rd and 24th of September to do some media coverage.

KENNESAWTAYLOR

The James Dean Of Dogs

I've had a good couple years of walking my dogs, three times a day. I need the exercise, so it's a good thing, right? I think my Grandpa would call it looking at the southbound end of a northbound mule. So, now we understand what walking a dog is like, Ok?

With all that to ponder, here's my point. Dogs have very distinct ways of walking. Mine are Australian Shepherds and are nicknamed as a breed, wiggle butts. (They don't have a tail, so they have to wiggle something.) They live up to it every day. The girl, Tillie, has a Marilyn Monroe little strut.

She takes care of her doggie business and looks around at me, "I can't believe I did that on the side of the road, Mr. President." she seems to say with her eyes and then prisses her little fanny on down the road.

My boy, Cape, on the other hand has the strut of John Wayne. He stands up real erect, with his head held high and kind of swaggers along. He has to have something about a foot deep to take care of his doggie business. In the summer time grass does just fine, but in the winter, he has to go quite a few blocks to come up with something that puts him in the mood. A fallen branch works sometimes or a big pile of leaves in the ditch. Poor thing has had a few accidents with briars. I think he's learned that lesson.

"How ya like that poopie pardner?" he seems to say and then swaggers off with his John Wayne gait, but he's only too happy to get back to the hot or cold house and hit the old couch again.

I've seen the hobo dogs. I swear their coats even look like hobo clothing. They move along with their heads down, trying to draw as little attention as they can. Usually, they're not that bad and just appreciate a hand out. They also know exactly where to show up and when to get the best handouts. If you follow one of these dogs, you'll find that he drifts from one store or house to another, possibly stopping by a restaurant or two as the day goes on.

The other day I saw the James Dean of dogs. He was a block or so ahead of us as we walked along. He had the haircut right. He looked like a small Great Dane, only with a James Dean haircut. His front legs were longer than his back, he looked fast and powerful. He'd hold his head up and test the air for my dog's scents, then like some thoroughbred, he'd move forward with the attitude of a rising, young star. Through it all his head was raised, giving him the appearance of royalty. After hesitating briefly, he'd go on a little farther. This went on for several blocks, he was something to watch. I'd never seen him before and haven't seen him since.

One of our neighbors walks their dogs about the same time we do. I think they're Miniature Dachshunds, foo foo dogs. Their bodies don't even move when they run to keep up with their owners. Their little, short legs just move in a blur and you think you should be hearing notes on a harpsichord when they run. Add to that they think they're ten feet tall and built like Rambo and you kind of get the picture of them.

I guess what all this means is, I know a little more about the southbound end of a northbound dog than I should.

A Big Fat Doggy Head

I guess you should understand that my dogs are herders. This and their affection for us makes them stay as close to us as possible when we're at home. Let's define close. When you walk in the door, there is this big, fat, dog head right up against your leg. Down the hall you go, with a dog head rubbing on the side or back of your legs. In the bathroom, there stands this dog booty for you to conveniently pet while you, well.

In the kitchen, you almost trip over them every time you back away from the stove or sink. You high step or side step to get to anything while you cook. It's almost impossible to put on your socks and shoes. No, that's not it, it is impossible to put them on. Remember that trick when you were young, where you stand behind someone and bump them in the back of their knee. Yeah, they do that all the time. You've got to be pretty sure footed to survive at our house. If you're in a hurry, they can tell and will walk along in front of you, trying to get you to stop and pet them.

They know when you're mad, sad or just upset and won't leave you alone until you give up and smile. If it's real cold, you can count on waking up to a big, fat, dog head in your bed. When a storm comes in, they know it an hour before and you can't even sit down without sitting on a big, fat, dog head. I guess I'm lucky I'm a little fond of those two heads or they would really annoy me.

Oh yeah, if you see someone walking two dogs down the road while they struggle to free themselves so they can doublehandedly, I know it's not a word, chase down and play with every squirrel

in Wilkinson County, it's me. Toot your horn, I'll
wave.

KennesawTaylor

The Dog Jones Industrial

I don't know if it's true for the rest of the Country or not, but where I live the dog is an economic indicator. The fate of the dog is so tied with ours that you can see a direct correlation between the economy and the dog. First, let's define the dog.

You have foo foo dogs. They're the ones that generally are balls of fluff or perhaps a small, hot dog with legs. They waddle along on their leashes, feet moving rapidly to keep up with their owners, whom often times seem similar to them. They serve no purpose with the exception of being doted on by their owners and to produce a byproduct that so far, no one has been able to find a market for. On top of that, in some neighborhoods, you actually have to pick said byproduct up after they produce it.

Then you have the working dogs. Since there are no sheep and few goats in my area and the cows are in the union, which doesn't allow them to work with dogs, they've never had jobs in the first place, talk about an economic crisis. I have two dogs that fit into this category. They don't seem to mind not having a job too much. In fact, we never let them in on the fact that they're dogs at all. I hope they don't read this, it would be a big shock to them. They are relegated to being large foo foo dogs and mostly lay around in the air conditioning and bark at the occasional squirrel that plays in the dogwood tree sitting in front of our house. Being perpetually unemployed is tough.

Then you've got the guard dogs. They run around your yard and bark at anything that annoys them, basically annoying you and your neighbors in the process. Many of them have jobs as lookouts and sentinels for drug dealers, a job that continues to prosper no matter the state of the economy.

Then there are the hunting dogs, which run through the woods hot on the tail of some animal who is scared out of its mind while rednecks with guns are hot on theirs. Wait a minute, I do that. My dogs probably hope I'm not reading this.

Then you have the most rapidly expanding kind of dogs, the homeless ones. They roam the streets of your neighborhood and turn over garbage cans. They harass foo foo dogs while they attempt to produce the product that all dogs produce that has no discernable market. They bark, chase and even bite you when you try to take out your trash and scare the mess out of you when you go outside at night. They are the first sign that the economy is bad because their numbers grow rapidly when it goes south.

Now I imagine that all dogs suffer when the economy slows down. Their treat selection is the first to suffer. Ours went from a large cabinet from the floor to the ceiling in our kitchen to one shelf in the same cabinet. If the truth be known, they haven't lost anything and they now have fresher treats than they did before. Our treat cabinet has taken the brunt of the slow down. They may have noticed a slight difference in the temperature of their environment because we adjusted our thermostat due to the price of electricity. It's a little bit hotter in the summer and a little bit cooler in the winter. Looking at them on the couch, which they actually believe in their hearts that they own, I don't think they've noticed at all. They still get to watch Wheel of Fortune every night.

They may have to deal with a few fleas, since the flea meds get stretched a little further apart now, but scratching fleas gives them something else to do as they are currently unemployed anyway. You know, now that I think about it, the economy hasn't changed my dog's life much. Now instead of rib eye and ham steaks, which they only got one bite of, we eat ham hocks and neck bones. We get less and their portions are bigger. One of them just looked at me and smirked, I swear.

Even the hunting dogs are getting a break. With the price of gas being more per gallon than beer, hunters don't actually go hunting anymore, but hang out at the watering hole closest to their homes and drink, leaving the dogs to lay around in the back of the truck, their main function being an alibi for their owners. If you asked the wives, they would probably tell you they were just glad their husbands are out of the house and the dogs are out of the yard.

I guess dogs really aren't economic indicators at all, just dogs. No matter how much I like mine, they all still have only one thing in common, you put money in one end and, well, you get the idea.

Shipwrecked Kitties

I never cared much for cats, but that all changed four years ago. I bought an old boat and let it sit for three days at my business, in the cold of March in the North Georgia Mountains. I then decided to fogger bomb the cabin to make sure nothing else was living in there before I went in. I tend to overdo things, so I had to use two bombs. As soon as the bombs stopped their eerie hissing, I heard the meowing of kittens inside. Now, while I didn't want bugs or snakes to greet me when I went in, kittens were another thing altogether.

Frantically I kicked out windows and holding my breath, I entered the cabin. The air was thick with the poison and I choked as I searched. I proceeded to destroy what was left of the inside of the boat. Becoming disorientated, I was unsure I would get back out the door. A friend arrived and pulled me to safety. Then he saved the two little black kittens as well. I put them in a box and closing the office that serviced the five businesses I owned, I headed for the vet.

"Their eyes aren't even open yet." the vet said. "They're dehydrated, almost frozen and now you've done a pretty good job of poisoning them. Just leave them to me, they can't possibly live."

I never even considered his suggestion. In fact, we may have changed vets over this. Instead I bought the supplies needed to bottle feed them for eight weeks. By the time eight weeks were up, I loved cats, or at least those two. We named them Gilligan and Ginger as they had been shipwrecked. My wife fed them at night, my secretary and I took turns all day, they went to work with me.

We took hundreds of pictures, as they struggled to survive and even though they were iffy, they pulled through. We were told all along as they got their shots and grew, that they would never live to be old cats. Their eyes were crossed and they didn't see well, but other than that, they were great cats. My admiration for cats grew as they went from barely filling the palm of my hand to being actually quite large. Our dogs thought they were their pups and took care of all the dirty work; we have too many pictures of that, too.

Gilligan sat in my lap and watched television most nights. Ginger was aloof, they ruled the house together, reigning over us and the dogs, all in all not a bad thing. Then about a year ago Gilligan started to lose weight. We took him to the vet, who was perplexed. We tried changing his diet and did so several times. Each time we tried something new he would rally for a time, but soon he would go back to losing weight and throwing up.

Antibiotics, vet visits and diet changes slowed down the process, but we watched as the year went by, him shrink smaller and smaller. He acted like he was hungry all the time, but ate continuously and his loving attitude never changed, he was the sweetest animal in the house. He lost his fight last Saturday and died in my wife's arms. I wasn't there and I regret it. He is buried in a pretty, little spot in our yard that my wife picked out.

This proves that you are never too old to change. It proves that every living soul has the power to make us better people. I never cared much for cats, but that changed four years ago. Thank you Gilligan.

THE GOOD OL' DAYS

Hog Killin Weather

With the way the heat is getting to us right now, I thought it a good time to talk about hog killin weather. It generally happens in the fall, but anytime during the winter will work. It must simply be cold enough outside to get the job done without letting the meat go bad in the process. We could all use a little hog killin weather right now. I guess it doesn't happen much anymore, but I remember when it was a yearly ritual.

Many family members and the neighbors that had nothing to do would show up at my grandparent's house. Several tables would be placed end to end in the yard. All the pots, pans, lard cans, knives, wrapping paper and black iron kettles needed to do the job were placed in the right spots along the table. The hog, who had been working hard all year just to build up the weight to be lucky enough to be selected, was escorted to one end of the table, at my grandparent's house it was always more than one. In the early years I think they killed it with a hammer, not a memory I want to go into detail about. After a while a rifle took that job, I was glad when it did. I think the hammer was a leftover from the depression.

The hog would be hung on a hook and cut into sections. Then he would start his way down the tables. The adults would cut and prepare the meat into all those hog things we love. Bacon, hams, ham steaks, roasts, pork chops, ribs and there were even a few dedicated to making sausage. Every piece was used, including the stomach, brains, skin, tongue and chitterlings. I know that looks like it's spelled wrong, but that's it. Cracklings were made, souse and head cheese, too. Some meat was hung to be smoked in an old smokehouse in the yard.

The kids ran up and down the table taking the fat to a large kettle at the end of the set up to be rendered into lard. Those of us old enough to remember this will smile thinking about it, those not old enough may get sick. In some way this was like a great family reunion. You saw family members you hadn't seen all year. As the meat moved along this ancient assembly line, it was prepared while it moved. It was separated and packaged before it slipped off the end of the tables and went into the freezer. Once everything was cleaned up and put away, the job was done, it took all day. Many of the men would be drunk by the time it was over.

You finished the job with more than a little blood on you and tired as all get out. This set of grandparents had a hog farm and ate hog three times a day all their lives, much of it salt cured. I guess the only reason they lived so long was because nobody told them it would kill you. Not only did they eat hog, but there was also hog in every dish. The lard was used as cooking grease and small pieces used to season vegetables. Even the corn bread was cooked in lard, the biscuits made with it. When you went to their house there was pig on the plate. Every holiday they killed a hog. Where else did cooking a pig come from? Eating pig and drinking was a part of life. I'm sure glad nobody told them how bad all that was for them, they lived to be quite old.

I remember sitting on the tailgate of grandpa's truck as he moved across the farm slowly. My cousins and I would slowly spread five-gallon buckets of corn in the road. From the front of the truck he would sing out in a voice so loud it could be heard all over the farm, "Sooouuuueeee, sooouuueee, pig," he would yell while we tried to imitate him from the back of the truck. As we crawled along, all 400 hogs would fall into line behind the truck for supper. This would probably pain some if it were one of their memories, not me. These were indeed the good old days. The days before you knew what was waiting for you in adulthood. The days when people got things done because no one told them they couldn't do it. A time before people died from eating too much pork, simply because they didn't know any better.

I'll never stop hearing my grandpa yelling from the cab of that truck and the way all those hogs came a runnin. Truth be told, there was probably a big jar of corn liquor on the front seat beside him all the while. I look forward to hog killin weather every year as I look forward to the planting season. Both are just memories for the most part, but I can feel and smell it in the air every year no matter how old I get.

Sweet Memories

I was at the fall line festival this weekend and found it funny when they did the ceremony to recognize our past and present veterans. Not that it was funny, in fact it was quite touching. However, right in the middle of this somber presentation a train slipped by on the tracks and as is their custom to do, it's whistle echoed through the night interrupting the ceremony, somehow it seemed right and reminded me of simpler times while we waited for it to pass so we could continue.

My wife moved from Kearney, Nebraska to Gordon with her mother & 4 brothers and sisters, while her Dad & oldest brother drove in the family car with their newest addition to the family, a Saint Bernard puppy named Duke. The last train they rode into Gordon on was the Nancy Hanks and it let them out at the station in Gordon. She spent the early years of her life here in Gordon. Coming back has been like a walk down memory lane. Memories like her uncles, Gerald and Kent Layton and Chuck Renaud, all having dune buggies and taking turns strapping the kids into them and going to Green Hills just to scare the mess out of them in general. Climbing a big pine tree that still stands in the parking lot of the new fire department and being too scared to come back down. I think the fire department had to go up and get her. I don't know who the fireman was, but thanks, I'd never had met her in that tree..

Memories of walking to church with the family at First Baptist Church and of her and all the neighborhood kids riding on their big Saint Bernard named Duke, like a horse. Cutting through the swamp barefoot and coming out just past the radio station, close to Aunt Betty's house to go to the

Gordon swimming pool where they always had a season pass, and the long summer days spent swimming there with all her family and friends. Memories of her first kiss, it was Allen Harris I think, and they were both too young to understand what it meant.

Sure, she was innocent, she was real young, but Gordon was innocent too. That lovely theater that sits downtown in a shambles was still operating and the future looked bright for Gordon. I hope there is success in bringing back the theater in some fashion so we can all enjoy it.

Still, her best memory involves trains. Freeman Brooks, her uncle, was an engineer for the railroad. On any given day he could be seen leaning out the window of one of those mammoth beasts, pushing or pulling train cars through Gordon. The roar of all that horsepower and the breathing and belching of the engine as it worked made quite an impression on the children of Gordon, it still does. Every time she was near the tracks he would wave and blow that whistle to beat the band. A sound so loud it actually runs through your body when you're that close.

She would stand there and wave until her little arm hurt, her little innocent face beaming with a bright smile only a very small child can muster. She was so very proud that her uncle was doing this for her and made sure all the other kids knew just how proud she was and that he was her uncle. These were some of her sweetest memories. She can still remember all the pennies that got laid out on the tracks & looking for them to save as souvenirs.

With age comes wisdom and it was some years before she realized that it was company policy to blow that old whistle in such a manner every time he crossed a road in town. What's more he probably blew it every time he saw a group of kids and might never have been able to see she was in the crowd at all. Still, the look that crosses her face when she hears a train whistle, even today is priceless. She still has that innocent six year old face and in that soft lost in thought look that comes over her face, you can still see that six year old little girl. She knows the facts, but the memory is still as sweet. She will always hold a special place in her heart for Freeman and for that old train whistle that blew many a time just for her and for Gordon, Georgia which is her home town, regardless of where she was born.

Ten Cents Worth Of Gas

I remember the first time I had any dealings with gas. I was eight and my father sent me to the store with a quart, mason jar without the lid and a dime. I walked the half-mile to downtown Blitchton, Ga. All the streets were dirt, but one. The only reason it was paved was because it just passed through, headed somewhere else. I was to get a jar full of gas for the lawn mower. By the time I got back I only had a half jar, spilling it everywhere, including on myself. Times sure have changed; today they'd take your kids away for doing that.

I went into the store and paid my dime. Returning to the pump, I found that the jar would only hold six cents worth. So I went back inside and got four cents worth of penny candy. Those days are gone and now they seem more like a Twilight Zone episode.

I started driving daily at 14, simply because I needed to. Growing up in Milledgeville, we used to take a spin around the Dairy Queen and then drive all the way out to McDonalds by the Hatcher Square Mall. We'd take a spin around it and then just do that same circuit about 400 times a night. I did it for two years before I even had a license. Back then, you could accomplish this very important social requirement for about five bucks a night.

Now, it takes five bucks just to get to the store to buy fifty bucks worth of gas. I know that it takes millions of years to make oil. I know we're going to run out. Still, I also know that all the high, gas prices are simply about greed. We are a captive audience and have no chance against the corporate greed that constantly takes advantage of us. It makes me ill when I think of the huge profits being made from us by large companies around the world. Before you start blaming every Country where Camels are indigenous, realize that many of the oil mongers are here in our own Country.

The powers that be are the ones that taught all those around the world to exploit Americans in mass, years ago. Our industry and government leaders are pulling many of the strings around the world that make us jump and dance. When will it end? Why would it? They jack the price of gas to over five bucks a gallon, then drop it to three so we feel like we're getting a bargain. People then rush out and buy gas guzzling SUV's to celebrate the drop.

It's partly our own stupidity. The advertising companies sold us water years ago and we still buy it. In a Country that has the cleanest water on the planet, we consume millions of bottles of water, at about four bucks a gallon. It's been proven that it takes three gallons of water to make one gallon of bottled water. What hasn't been proven, is that the bottled water is any better. Still we keep on buying. In all the Countries I've visited there are few where the water doesn't fill your bowels with parasites that make you deathly ill, ours is one of them. Our water systems are legendary all over the world; bottled water was designed for those other Countries. What happened?

Why are we surprised that the price of gas has finally outreached the price of water? Ok, that's too crazy to even talk about, proving that even my insanity has limits. I wonder if soon we'll be able to go to the store and pump out 10 cents worth of water into a quart mason jar.

Super Chicken and Employee Locked in Battle to the Death

I don't know about you, but with my wallet getting thinner due to the economy, fast food is becoming more of a necessity. Against the wishes of my wife and doctor, I might add. I swear I think one or both of them are watching from the bushes every time I eat something I'm not supposed to. I remember when fast food was a chicken nobody could catch. Every week on chicken night I chased it around, but it continued to elude me and my siblings. Sooner or later Dad would get involved. You could see it in his beady, little eyes that he knew his career in fast food was over. Sitting at the table eating the chicken in question, you had a feeling that you'd beaten him. It made the food taste better, somehow.

Then fast food did appear on the scene. Many fought against it, but in my lifetime we've become a nation of junk food junkies. I grew up with it and it became a big part of my life. When I graduated from boot camp, while in the Navy, I was asked where I wanted to eat. I could have had a steak, could have went anywhere I wanted, but a Big Mac was my choice. In fact I think I ate two. Spending much time overseas before the fast food restaurants made it over there, I missed all the hamburgers I'd gotten used to and salivated thinking about returning to America for them. On those long nights at sea standing watch, we would sit and talk about all the fast food joints and which one we were going to hit first when we touched American soil. Well, girls may have been the most popular subject, but hamburgers were right up there with them. Once the ship was tied up and everything shut down, I was headed for a fast food joint. Sure, I was glad to see my wife, she had the car that would take me to McDonalds.

Standing in a line the other day for breakfast I noticed several things. There was an older woman in front of me; I swear she had fear in her eyes as she contemplated dying from old age in line. Everyone there started making funny comments about how slow fast food had become. We laughed about it for thirty minutes and when all of us were gone that poor woman still hadn't gotten her food. She'd been in front of us all.

I must wonder if research on animal DNA has had an effect on fast food. Now we have super chickens, pigs and cows. Is it like chicken night when I was young? Are the employee's chasing around animals that can't be caught? Has there been some great digression in human evolution? It seems that the employees in fast food restaurants are dumber than ever, more likely they just don't care. They drag their feet and act like you're bothering them just by being there. If you go through the drive through, you can bet your order will be wrong and you'll have to go in anyway, making you late for work. The food is getting faster and the employees are getting slower, not a winning combination. The title of this story may be a headline one day. Super chicken and employee battle to the death as others look on, the chicken wins.

From what I can see, if you're going to be on time for work, you might as well go hungry. Were hooked now, but don't have the time to enjoy it except on the weekends, when we have enough time to wait for our favorite fast food. I don't know what happened, but fast is no longer an appropriate description and if you take away the fast all you're left with is junk.

The Days Of The Horse

News flash, the car has surpassed money as the root of all evil. People now spend more money on repairs, insurance, maintenance, taxes, accessories and payments on their cars than they do on their houses. Many will be surprised to find a traffic jam on the way into their eternal resting place, whether it be north or south.

Being in the car business years ago, I've seen many people that would steal from family, friends, employers or who even committed robberies to obtain and maintain a nice car, all things that have always been connected with drug addiction. The difference however, is that the federal government hasn't declared war on the automobile industry. You don't hear about the Coast Guard searching ships trying to stop the flow of them into the Country. The government hasn't developed programs for people with car problems such as Automobiles Anonymous or even pamphlets on how to kick the car habit. There are no pills or fancy gadgets to wean you off of the car. I can't do without one, but at least my old truck has over three hundred thousand miles on it and I'll drive it until the wheels fall off. I shouldn't say that, it may hear me and die of old age in its sleep, while I'm writing this.

In fact, at the time of writing this they're getting ready to give the car industry billions of dollars so they can pay people an average of twenty seven dollars an hour to sweep floors in a plant that produces a product people who make ten dollars an hour or less, have to pay for. Don't get me wrong, if I could figure out a way to make ten dollars an hour writing, I'd have a new truck in my driveway.

People get divorced, assault each other, mistreat their kids and even kill over their cars, but nothing is done. Come on, wake up, these people need help. Where's all the support for them? The government is involved in everything else. The automobile even creates much of the pollution on our planet. What are we going to do about it? We're so hooked at this point, that most households own more cars than they have people to drive them.

Whether it's the government, as some think or merely the finance institutions, someone is determined to keep us all in debt. The automobile has long surpassed the house as the number one thing most financed. Many that pay $600.00 car payments or more every month, live in shacks they don't even own. At one dealership, I made the biggest deal that had ever been made there. I waited naturally; until the customer signed all the papers (I'm only slightly stupid), then I asked this question. You live in a trailer, in your parent's backyard and you just bought a car with $547.00 a month payments. What are you thinking? I'll never forget his answer, (you can sleep in your car, but you can't drive your house). He never paid the first payment on that car. In fact it had a flat tire shortly after he bought it that he couldn't even afford to replace. The car was repossessed soon thereafter, still sporting that donut spare.

Show me a person with bad credit and I'll show you a person who couldn't afford the car he bought, that started him in a downward spiral in the first place. I know we can't live without them, but we surely must learn to control them instead of it being the other way around. Give me a good old horse any day.

TRANSPORTATION

I'm a Skippin if You're a Poppin

If it was just me, well I might understand. I used to climb on my grandpa's old tractor when I was a very little boy and ride for hours while he plowed the large corn field next to the house, a field where he grew the corn to feed his pigs for the winter. It was fun for me and when I was older and had to do it alone. I figured out it made it better for him, too. He had someone to talk to, I'm telling you right now, plowing 40 acres by yourself is like watching cars rust, and it's boring as all get out.

What I've found is, just like trains, people have an infatuation with tractors. This infatuation is intensified the older the tractor is. The Skippin and Poppin tractor show at the Fall Line Festival in Gordon further proves it. There were tractors of all sizes, shapes and colors. Some were so carefully restored and tended to that they gleamed in the sunlight. Others were just everyday work tractors, simply being given the day off to attend the show, but some were the ugliest old specimens of a tractor you've ever seen. These seemed to garner the most attention.

During the parade there were itty bitty tractors driven by young children. Everyone wanted to ride on one, the route was lined with spectators who wanted to watch and listen to the old tractors skip and pop along. I had a booth and couldn't go watch all the competitions that occurred throughout the day, but I bet I do next year, for like everyone else that was there I have a fascination with old tractors. Why is beyond my understanding. Maybe it's like the train. They signify all that is pure about our Country. Men who use tractors have been the salt of the earth throughout time. Unsung heroes that work hard and at the deepest level keep this Country going, men who pioneered this Country. The men who made this nation the nation that feeds the world.

Many songs have been written about the tractor in the last decade and have become big commercial hits. I have a friend, a woman named Tracey French and she loves anything with John Deere on it, she collects everything John Deere. It's down right baffling and cute at the same time.

My father-in-law tells the story about him and his brothers climbing on a combine in the forties and driving south of their Nebraska home until they found a place south enough where the wheat was ready to harvest. Arriving at their first job, they had a little water, a little coffee and just a small chunk of bread. Then they followed the harvest back north for a couple of months, hiring themselves out, combining, thrashing and hauling to market for three bucks an acre until they arrived back home in time to harvest their own wheat. They drove that sucker right down the road for hundreds of miles, three young men hanging on wherever they could get a hold on, trying to make a little money for their family during extremely hard times. They slept on the ground under the combine and cooked on the exhaust system the entire time. They endured severe rain storms and had much difficulty, but in the end it was a grand adventure for them.

So on Saturday when Lynne Watson asked me the now famous question: Do you want to ride my big green tractor? I was in and enjoyed riding on Vernon Watson's tractor in the parade. The Gordon

Fall Line Festival was a great success and of course the Skippin and Poppin show was a big part of that. I'd like to take this time to thank Ryan Mitchner and everyone who had a hand in it. Ryan I look forward to seeing what you do for next year. This one was amazing, I can only imagine what you'll do with a whole year to prepare.

KENNESAW TAYLOR

Spanish Airlines

Now I wouldn't want you to think sailors drink a lot, but I might have. One night when I returned to the ship, I was escorted to the Captain's quarters. Not a good thing at three AM intoxicated. To top it off, no one would tell me what was going on. I realized that something was wrong and thought of my mom at once. I didn't know my Dad, so he never crossed my mind. I almost laughed when they told me he'd had a heart attack. I don't say this with disrespect; I was just relieved that it wasn't my Mom. I could've laughed, but it would've looked bad.

Anyway, it seemed that the Red Cross found me and I was faced with the problem of getting to Texas with no money. The Red Cross had everything covered. They'd arranged 30 days leave and a five hundred dollar loan including a plane ticket. I needed a vacation anyway and always wanted to know my Dad. So I acted upset, grabbed the ticket and stumbled downstairs to pack my stuff.

Within the hour I was at the San Diego airport in the bar, waiting for my plane. I had a couple of drinks and stumbled onto the plane. I had a few more drinks there and passed out. When we arrived I had one heck of a hangover and was sick. I know you've heard the saying (hair of the dog that bit him). I had, so I did. I fell into the first bar I found and had a few drinks to try and feel better, figuring I couldn't feel any worse. After an hour layover in Dallas I found out I was wrong. I felt like I'd been run over by a truck. To make matters worse, a storm came up and the flight from Dallas to Galveston had been delayed, so I passed out again.

It was still early in the morning. It'd only been a few hours since I was drinking in San Diego.

I'd been drinking ever since and had only slept briefly. I really just wanted, no, needed to die. However, I couldn't give up. After all, they'd said he didn't have long to live. So I dragged myself to the plane and boarded.

The flight from Dallas to Galveston is a short one, about 45 minutes. The plane was a little 2 engine, 30 passenger job with the name of the Airline painted on the tail with a brush. The pilot looked too young and a little scared. Even as miserable as I was, I still noticed things. The flight attendants were older and I was fighting the urge to laugh at the whole situation. The thing I'd failed to notice at this point was the fact that everyone on the plane, except for the pilot, one stewardess and myself, spoke only Spanish.

Now I'm not a pilot, but I knew the take off wasn't supposed to be that rough. We took off into a storm the likes of which I'd never flown in before. I'd been through a lot and was still drunk, so I figured I could handle it. I would have too, but the Hispanics started to get alarmed. Spanish is fast normally, but you get a plane full of people together that think they're going to die and it goes supersonic. I heard the pilot tell the only other English speaking person on the plane to get buckled in and ask the Hispanic stewardess to calm the passengers down. The American woman sat down and strapped herself in. The Spanish woman tried to calm the passengers, but only seemed to stir them up more. She then joined the other woman. It was everyone for themselves.

That was the longest 45 minutes of my life. I sobered up and quit drinking 15 times. The pilot probably quit his job as many times. Both flight attendants probably retired and 10 Spanish-speaking people were born again. It only took God about twenty more tries to teach me a lesson about drinking, but this was the first and most impressionable one.

KENNESAWTAYLOR

The Railroad Runs Through it

People who live near the railroads that cross our Country are quick to complain about them. There are plenty of things to complain about. The noise, the smell, the traffic delays are familiar to us all. Still, America holds them in a special place, a romantic place, real or imagined. Trains made it possible for people to travel across the Country safely and quickly, back when they were new. They made or destroyed towns based on their routes. It seems that the railroad has followed me my entire life.

I've lived on or near the rail most of my life, sometime on the right, but many times on the wrong side. The railroad has a way of dividing towns in such strange ways. In my youth I cared little about which side I lived on. I remember when I was young; there were circus trains that passed occasionally. They would speed by with their brightly, colored cars headed to some distant town, one that undoubtedly was bigger than any I ever lived in. They never stopped, but just passed us by.

I've been to 37 Countries in my life and found this to be true in all of them. I rode the street cars in San Francisco, the Orient express in several Countries. The Tokyo subway, the New York subway and rode the train to the top of Victoria Peak in Hong Kong. People the world over love a train.

I've walked a million miles on gravel and railroad ties. I always thought I was going somewhere, but never really did. At some point it would be supper time and we'd turn back. That's what the rail represents; people sit on their front porch and watch the train speed by, thinking about all the places they've never been or all the places they'll never go.

I've came back home as a child many times, holding a spike in my dirty little hands. Later as a mechanic, I had one in my tool box thinking someday I'd use it for something. I never did. I still have one in my tool box today; I've been carrying it for years. Tell me that's not crazy.

In North Carolina you can take a trip on the mystery train. It's like a game of Clue on a train, it's a lot of fun. On our 20th anniversary we went there and had dinner on a train as it eased through the countryside. I had to dress in a suit and tie; my wife had to wear a fancy dress. It was elegant and the food was rich and delicious. This trip was well worth the money we paid for it. You should check it out.

Still, what struck me the most about this trip was the scenery. It travels through the mountains, but at night, so you don't see the beauty of the valleys you're passing through. It was designed that way, because the houses and towns you pass through are some of the poorest places in the state. Looking out the windows, mostly you see darkness, but where there are lights, you see poverty. It's a strange feeling to be eating prime rib, Beef Wellington and drinking champagne as you move through places from your past in the present.

It was a humbling experience; we came away with a feeling worth far more than the meal and ride we paid for. We were inspired to take a few days to travel by car to the places the train had taken us. That ride was even more humbling, we'll never forget it.

I've been lucky to have the life I've had and lucky that a railroad runs through it.

Why I Drive Old Junk

I have reasons. My standard answer is, I was in the car business. They're not worth what you pay for them. The real answer, I only paid four hundred dollars for my old truck. That's less than your down payment and close to your monthly payment. My insurance is cheaper and no monthly payment. If I drop a cigarette in the floor, it doesn't cause me to curse all day, pray all night and attend therapy all month. If an older person in town runs into it, I can say it's only a scratch, don't worry about it, you just have a good day. Much better than blessing out somebody. However, if some idiot cuts me off or muscles in on me in traffic, he can do his worst. If you've seen my truck, you understand. They have more to lose than I do.

I like it that sometimes, as God does, old cars make you stop and slow down. You wake up after not sleeping well; you drink too much coffee, too fast. Your heart is beating wildly, you're convinced that you're forgetting something and you know it will ruin your day. Then it happens, the truck won't start. Now, when I was younger I would go ballistic, cursing loudly and throwing things. I might even go ten rounds with the truck. I would lose, I always did.

How funny that must have been to God, sitting up there watching something he meant to slow me down, turn me into an idiot. I do hope he enjoyed all the times (and there were many) it took for me to learn his lesson. Most times now I smile, scratch my head and get out my tools. While I fix the truck I reassess my situation in life and by the time it's fixed, I feel better about life in general.

There's also something to be said about driving something that you've worked on. When I used to race, the feeling of driving something that I built with my own hands was much more important than winning with it.

Driving old junk has taught me many things in life that more of us should know. It's given me opportunities to reevaluate my life in my yard, as well as and on the side of the road.

Later in life, my truck broke down on a section of Ga. I-16 where there were no exits for miles. Traffic was slow and at the nearest exit, the stations were closed. We were still two hours from home and I wasn't about to leave my truck on the side of the road. It was loaded down with tires, tools and all the expensive junk that goes along with racing. Hooked to the back was the trailer with the race car on it.

The only cars on the road were coming from the races, so soon a fan stopped who lived near us. He agreed to take the kids home, loaned us a flashlight and let us use his cell phone. My brother had left town with my other truck, so he was no help. I assured them we were OK. After all, we had a whole extra car on the trailer with all the tools and extra parts we could need.

We sat in the truck, quietly considering the problem. Shortly we got out, took parts off the car, putting them on the truck, until we fixed it. We were there for two hours. On that lonely highway, that old truck we'd named Fred taught us a lot. Not about old trucks, but about life's lessons. When we got it running, we drove to the house with a good feeling about life. We had a story to tell for weeks; actually years it would seem. I had been talking the talk, but that night I caught a glimpse of the walk. I think God was smiling and I smiled with him. Why do I drive old junk? The real answer is because I can and before long we may all be doing it out of necessity. Hey, good thing, I've been practicing for years.

KENNESAWTAYLOR

Announcing the Ivey Vienna Sausage 500

Nascar is pleased to announce the addition of a new track and a new venue for their 2010 season. The track, formally known as the streets of Ivey, has been preparing for years. "All that's needed is to add some grandstands in a few front yards and we're ready," says their official spokesman for Nascar in Wilkinson County R. U. A. Moron. Anyone will be allowed to race, but there are a few rules specific to this area that they want published.

Fenders must still be attached by at least one bolt. One headlight must be still in place, even if held on by duct tape, taillights are optional. If your windshield isn't already cracked, you might want to pre crack it before the race. Mufflers, as always, are optional.

Driver's rules: Helmets are not required as no brain damage is possible. A ball cap preferably turned sideways is recommended. The driver must prove with some reasonable doubt that they have at least two brain cells. If they can't prove it, then more drivers may be added to the car to bring the total number of brain cells to 2, limit 10 people per car. All cars must have at least three kids in them hanging from the windows. There must be an extra person whose job is to throw trash from the windows while the car careens through the neighborhood throughout the entire race. Running out of trash before the race ends will result in immediate disqualification. The music coming from the car must be emanating from a poor quality sound system and if someone on the course doesn't hear the words train, truck and at least seven cuss words from your car, you will also be disqualified. The driver must pass a drug test, they must be able to identify and be in possession of at least five different varieties.

All point rules for Nascar will be followed with the following additions: Each dog hit while being walked on a leash will count as 2 points, 3 if it belongs to someone who cares for it, only 1 point will given for hitting a dog who regularly runs the neighborhood freely. Innocent children in the streets will score 5 points each, all other pedestrians will merely score 1 point. Writers come in at a whopping 10 points each. Good news, every newspaper within 200 miles will be covering the race. Each car must complete the race with at least one road sign in the backseat.

Ok, I crossed that line again, here's the thing. Two dogs have been hit on my street in the last year while on a leash attached to their owners. I'm sure it was the owner's fault, since they had their dogs on a leash, but they swear that the cars went out of their way to hit the dogs. Everybody's always looking for someone to blame, but don't try to blame it on the Ivey P.D. They'd have to have 400 officers to keep it from happening. They can only do so much.

Now for a statement. If you hit my dogs, you'll have to hit me. I keep mine on a short leash. I hope that a writer counts enough to get you locked up, but we might not. I forgot Stephen King was run over while walking near his home in Maine a few years ago. Maybe a better thing to say is, if you hit my dogs you better hit me. If you don't, the car you're driving will never hit another dog. If you get out, you stand a pretty good chance of never hitting another one yourself. I might be as guilty of this as anyone, but I don't generally take curves on two wheels or drive dirt bikes at 75 miles an hour without a helmet.

At least this will stop soon, because eventually someone is going to run over an innocent child and then maybe the community will slow down out of some sense of rational thinking that isn't apparent at the moment. I hope that isn't what it'll take for this to stop.

KENNESAW TAYLOR

JUST FOLKS

Waltzing with Merle

"Shall we?" she raises her frail brown spotted hand, still feminine, almost too smooth.

"I think we shall." He takes her hand and lightly kisses it, the act alone bringing back memories of his childhood, memories of the woman his grandmother was in her youth.

As usual the walls are lined with the old, the forgotten, the ones who watch the doors everyday for a familiar face that never appears. His grandmother has been here for over a year and James has been here every week. His visits become more of a treat for all the residents in attendance. Softly, slowly the first notes of the song, The Dance, by Garth Brooks starts, as it has every week for many months. Gingerly he places her hand on her lap, a lap composed of legs that no longer do their job.

He places his hands on the handles of her chair, a chair that has become her prison, a chair that has become her only escape from the bed that is her life. No more kitchen to preside over, no more biscuits to make, no more booboos to kiss and make better. A bed, a few pictures and a few wind chimes that hang silently over her on the ceiling, this is her world now. This song, its words bring pain, but pain brings the reality that James still has his grandmother. The words symbolize the fact that he will endure this pain as long as it lasts to keep his memories of the better times alive as long as possible.

Slowly they move across the room towards Mrs. Bitterman, who's face is aglow with long ago dreams, her mouth hangs open in an almost dreamy smile, a tear slips down her overly rouged face. Just at the right moment James makes a turn and spins Merle around in ever increasing circles, back into the center of the room. Gracefully he spins her, sometimes he worries he's overdoing it, but the smile on her face and the school girl giggle confirms that he's doing the right thing. The excitement might one day kill her, but he knows it would be the best way for her to go. This too would guarantee that he be there in her last moments, moments he is afraid he'll miss.

The other residents sit and watch, smiling, some crying, but in joy, in remembrance of days that are long passed. Some move from the wall and spin around slowly in a circle thinking of their own James and wondering where he is and how his kids are doing. Mr. Cullpepper slowly moves across the floor staring towards the ceiling, a position he no longer has control of. Drool escapes his mouth, but it escapes from a smile.

The melody is glorious, the words are apt and the dance continues. James leans Merle back in a makeshift dip and the joy from her heart is evident on her face. His shoes make little squeaking sounds on the floor as he moves along, taking advantage of the whole room and attempting to make this dance the one she'll never forget. Just like he'll never forget all the dances he had with her as a child. Those are his memories, ones she no longer shares with him. This memory will only last a little while, but it's the most important one, right now, right here.

As it does every week, the song and the memories bring a lump to his throat, the tears start to flow and he dances through it. Below him Merle too is crying, but both are crying through smiles. As with every week, the attendants stand along the wall keeping an eye on the frail people, ever vigilant for problems, but they too weep, they too look forward to this dance. As the song comes to a close James slowly comes to a stop in the center of the room, moves in front of Merle and drops to his knees.

"I love you Grandmother, thanks for the dance."

There is no dry eye in the room, the normal response for their weekly dance. Her face is wrinkled, but he still sees the beautiful little girl in the pictures on his mantle. For a moment longer she is there, she is present, but then her eyes gray slightly, it's almost perceptible.

"Are we having pea soup for dinner? I so love peas soup."

"Yes grandmother, we're having pea soup." If there is pea soup or not is unimportant, she'll not remember pea soup in a matter of moments.

Who's Your Daddy

We had names before our son was born. When he arrived I began referring to my wife as mom, she referred to me as dad. So it went for twenty years. We might as well have not had names. We did it wherever we went and hardly noticed. Other kids referred to us as Randy's mom and dad, so did parents and teachers, just about everybody. It took us a while after he moved out to realize we were still doing it and had to make an effort to stop. Just when we were getting used to calling each other by our names again and if you've been through this you understand how hard that was, we got dogs.

We quickly slipped back into the mom and dad thing right away, not just a little, but all the way back to the sappy, sick, sweet, baby, mom and dads. Now we were Cape and Tillie's mom and dad at the vet, park and on the streets of our neighborhood. Our names slipped from us once again. This time I fear we'll call each other mom and dad for the rest of our lives, but check this out.

Don Green was born in Buffalo County, Nebraska. He was the son of the local, longtime postmaster whom had held several government positions over the years and in fact knew everybody in the state. Don went to college, came back home and helped improve the Buffalo County school system. He taught for eight years and then moved on to run a crew that helped spread roads throughout Nebraska. His family were farmers and he was one of the first to take advantage of the large water reserves that lay just below the surface of the region. This water turned Nebraska into the agricultural state that it is.

People from all over came to see his systems for lifting water and in fact his house was one of the first in the state to have gravity fed, indoor plumbing. Don's name soon became known all over the mid west, soon surpassing his father's notoriety.

His son, Myron Green, grew up in the shadow of all this and was known his whole life as Don Green's son. His name wasn't important; it was his dad's name that mattered. Myron Green is my father in law and I listened intently, as any dutiful son in law must, as he told me this story. He went to college and graduated at the age of seventeen, then went on to help run the family farm and business. He got married and had six children, naming his youngest son, Don Green, after his dad. Then he ended up moving to Georgia, his wife's neck of the woods. It wasn't until then that he stopped being known as Don Green's son.

He had a brief reprieve and then Don Green, his son, opened a business. Soon all in the County knew who Don Green was and Mr. Green became Don Green's dad. Now as he makes his rounds to the post office, to get breakfast, to the hardware store or anywhere else he must go, he is referred to as Don's dad. All employees at the store over the years and all their kids call him that, as well as all of Don's friends and customers. So far this has been going on for about twenty year's already and now that he's eighty, we hope it continues for a lot longer.

I thought it ironic and told him it was an unusual story.

"This is not an original story." he said. "When Amadeus Mozart was a child, his father was an important politician of the times. He grew up as Mozart's son. Later in life, after the younger Amadeus began to make a name for himself, the elder became Mozart's father and so it was until the day he died.

I doubt that Cape or Tillie will ever become a Mozart, but I guess it ain't half bad being known as Cape and Tillie's dad after all.

KENNESAWTAYLOR

Tommy Lightfoot

I grew up with Tommy Lightfoot. He was an American Indian and claimed that the only thing, other than his name he got from his dad was his prominent nose and a propensity to drink. He was my fishing buddy for a time.

The pond lay deep in the woods, far from the nearest road. I'd never been to it. The farmer who owned it preferred no one to fish in it, so those who dared were rewarded with the true meaning of fishing. Stories drifted around town of the spirited bass that could be caught there, they being well fed and strong. Not only were they big, but they could put up a hell of a fight.

"I don't know about this Tommy. What if we get caught?"

"Relax man, he'll never catch us, we're a long way from his house out here."

I looked behind us warily as we moved through the woods. The shadows from the trees above us played along our path. Tommy moved along stealthily ahead of me, only his wife's youngest brother, walking along between us separated us. Choo choo, they called him. He was only about six and quiet. Tommy had been charged with keeping an eye on him and he went fishing with us often. I loved kids, but failed in all my attempts to befriend this young boy. He was slightly towheaded and just oddly aloof.

He walked in front of me, head hung low, hardly paying attention to where he placed his feet. He stumbled occasionally; I reached out, steadied him and set him back on course. Soon we broke from the trees into a field of tall grass, it running off down hill towards the pond. The pond sitting at the base of a hill was large 10 acres possibly. Surrounded by a sea of yellow grass is sat there like a jewel. The water was turquoise and vast shade trees bordered its banks. One lone dock jutted into it from the right side.

The morning was cool, but just a bit, the birds sang in the trees and a rabbit skittered away from us in the grass as we moved through it towards the pond. This farmer had a little slice of heaven right here on his little part of the earth.

We moved down to and out onto the dock, having a seat.

"I could sit here forever."

"Me too," I said, leaning back and watching the clouds slip across the sky. Fishing isn't always about fishing, it's about talking and enjoying nature sometimes. Choo choo lay back and watched the sky as well, a simple smile danced on his face. It occurred to me that maybe being a little thick had some advantages. I'd never heard him complain, he had no cares, all in all he was a good-hearted kid.

"See that tree on the other side of the pond."

"Which one?" Tommy asked, sitting back up to see it.

"The one with all that brush under it."

"Yeah so?"

"I'm gonna go over there and pull a big ass bass out of this pond." I said.

"Good luck," He said.

I got my things together and made my way around the pond, fishing as I went along. Tommy and Choo choo sat and watched my progress. My catching a few small bass, that I threw back, made their decision for them. Tommy set up Choo choo on the dock and then moved off to attempt to catch the biggest fish of the day. I soon arrived at the appointed tree and started using my limited bass fishing techniques to do the same. The breeze blew the sweet smell of left over honeysuckle across the field, I could smell the yellow hay as the wind whipped at it. What a beautiful day I thought.

I caught what would have been a keeper, but threw it back. We had too far to walk to keep anything short of a stuffer. Tommy caught one on the other side of the lake that looked good. I caught and released three more. Choo choo caught one, he threw it on the dock and let it flop as he went back to fishing. Tommy caught another, held it up, threw it back and moved down the bank a little more.

I had a seat and watched from a distance as Choo choo caught the biggest so far. He held it high over his head and danced, the whole while smiling brightly. At that moment Tommy hooked a big one. I watch as he fought the fish trying to get it to the bank. This would be the biggest of the day fore sure. After what seemed like eternity he pulled it from the water. It was too big to lift into the air with the line, he'd done it. After unhooking it he lifted it high in the air in triumph. I shot him a thumbs up and watched as he turned towards the dock to Choo choo.

The fish fell from his hands in slow motion as he started to run slipping in the wet grass on the edge of the pond. Glancing towards the dock I saw Choo choo flailing in the water. I was too far away to be any factor in the outcome of what was happening, but I broke into a dead run instantly. My heart raced as I did so. I watched helplessly as Tommy dove into the water and swam past the dock frantically. I watched as he dragged Choo choo to the bank and worked desperately to revive him.

Tommy lay across his body crying as I fell into the mud beside them.

"He's dead." I checked his pulse, there was none. He lay there still looking simple, but at peace. Tommy picked him up and started to run back toward the woods the way we had come. I tried to keep up, but even in as good of shape as I was in he outdistanced me. When I broke from the woods, out of breath, his car was gone.

It was a long walk home, one that was infused with sadness for the simple little boy named Choo choo, who had never hurt anyone. With the sadness for my friend who had failed his small brother in law in the worst way and for his wife who doted on Choo choo. Tommy Lightfoot never spoke to me again, in fact he quit the job we shared and never even looked me in the eyes. The weight of his failure was too much for our friendship to bear.

Two weeks later the newspaper called it an accident. Tommy fell asleep at the wheel and hit a tree, killing himself instantly. His wife knew it wasn't true, I could see it in her eyes at the funeral. I knew it wasn't true, I could see it in his eyes that day that Choo choo lay there lifelessly in the mud. Tommy Lightfoot was my friend and for a time he was my fishing buddy.

Capin Bridges

This story could have been named Captain Bridges, past, present and future. It came about in the most unusual way, but we'll get to that soon enough. In researching Capt'n Bridges, (which is what everybody refers to him as), very little could actually be found. However, after talking to many Wilkinson County residents, it appears that everyone had a story to tell. He was a product of his time, doing a job that needed to be done and much the local hero. He ran the work camp on Hwy. 57 from the time it opened until it closed.

As with any person who is charged with such a job, he was at the heart of some controversy, the biggest being when a prisoner drowned in the pond behind the camp, while acting as a retriever for the good old boys shooting ducks. Soon after, three prisoners escaped and were able to make their way to Lester Maddox's office in Atlanta to file a grievance. They did, but were sent back. Governor Maddox did visit the prison. Many people thought that was the reason the work farm was shut down. It was shut down simply because they were in the process of shutting down all such facilities at the time.

The work camp raised hogs and planted acres of food. It was totally self-sufficient and did not rely on the State for anything. Anyone could just stop in and have lunch with the guards on any day. The reports from many say it was the best food you'd ever ate.

A local resident, Charles Jackson, remembered an open house he attended as a child. A hog was to be killed with a hammer. Several prisoners tried, with no success, to do it. Capt'n Bridges came out and instructed another to give it a try, using very colorful language. Bridges stood there and stared the pig down as the prisoner walked in and killed it with no problem. Even the pig knew who was the boss. "Capt'n Bridges was the definition of a correctional officer, once you got out of his camp, you were corrected." says Jackson.

Now to the present, one of the E.M.T.'s contacted me about an apparent haunting at the old work camp. After interviewing over a dozen people, the claim seems to have some merit. Many have been grabbed in the night, many have seen an apparition that wears a large brimmed hat, similar to the one that Bridges wore. Several gave exact statements about shared events. A crock-pot flew from the top of the refrigerator in front of several members at once. The stove continues to just turn itself on while they watch television. Getting a new stove didn't change that. Once while at a fire, the E.M.T.'s were in the back of the ambulance keeping cool. One watched through the window as the shifter went from park to drive, with no one in the front of the bus. Luckily when it started moving, a fireman noticed and jumped in to stop it. All night those sleeping there heard the jail doors open and slam. 'It's a very distinct sound,' one of them said, all doors in the old jail are locked with large padlocks.

One man, who wishes to remain anonymous, was there spending the night it was his first day on the job. He opened his eyes to see a figure with that old wide brimmed hat standing over him with a stern look on his face. He pulled the covers over his head and started yelling 'go away, go away' over and over. It woke up the entire station. That was his first and last night as a Wilkinson County E.M.T. The whole station as a rule, doesn't tell new people, so they can see how long it takes for them to meet the Capt'n.

One girl, the one who brought this to me, said she was grabbed the first night so violently that she kicked the zipper out of the bottom of the sleeping bag she was sleeping in and has had many encounters since.

Maybe the entire crew and all the past E.M.T.'s that have ever worked there are crazy, I don't think so. There is just too much information for me to believe that. Now, Wilkinson County has built a new building to house this service and the crew is slightly concerned that Bridges will follow them the three miles to their new home. Believe me, they hope he doesn't.

Since moving, the time is fast approaching that they will tear down that old work camp. I spoke to Alfred Bridges recently, Captain Bridges son, who lives in Gray. He remembers standing watch there as a 14-year-old, when guards would lay out. "If that place was haunted, I'd know," he said. Like me, he was sad to see it go and like me said he'd love to be there when it's torn down. He wants a brick from the building that consumed over thirty years of his father's life.

I have no idea if the Capt'n is still there, but I'll say this. If he is, then he deserves to be. He and inmates built it with their own hands, he and inmates built and maintained most of the bridges and roads in the County for years. It being before the county could afford expensive equipment, they dug most of the ditches in the county with shovels

"You best not write a story that makes the Capt'n look bad," was a quote that I got from untold numbers of Wilkinson County residents. He was looked up to as a great man in the community and was well respected. I don't know about the rest of you, but we could use a few thousand more like the

Capt'n. If we had them, the Country would be in much better shape.

KENNESAW TAYLOR

Merle Arthur

Merle Arthur was my grandmother or grandmaw, as I called her. She was a redneck cooker, but I'm not sure I could have told her that to her face. Even though I was in my thirties by the time she passed, I can say that she never saw me smoke, drink or cuss. She was a saint if there ever was one. Not the kind that would ever get recognized as one, but the everyday saint that worked hard, paid her bills, made a snotty nosed, little butthead like me feel loved and cooked some of the best food I've ever eaten. I've cooked upwards of a thousand pones of cornbread. Even though she taught me how to do it, none of them have ever compared to any she cooked over the years. Thank you grandmaw for all the years of love, biscuits and all you taught me about the right thing to do. I think of her every time I get a compliment on my cooking. After all, is it not a compliment to her? She was never the President or anything so grand as that, but she left behind a legacy that continues to thread through the lives of her children's children. I'll never forget you grandmaw or the part you played in making me the redneck cooker that I am.

Chuck Renaud

Chuck Renaud was my wife's uncle. Some of you may remember him, he ran Stevens Pottery for years. Later, he was a big wheel for Rodenberry in South Georgia. He was married to Sammie Layton from Gordon, Georgia. He also was an extraordinary cook, who could probably trace his cooking skills back to Wilkinson County, Georgia. After all, his wife's mother was one of the best cooks to ever step into a kitchen. He was my 'go to guy' for a while, whenever I was cooking something unusual. He and his son Charles cooked things like alligator and buffalo. Charles went on to have a cooking show on PBS. Thank you Chuck for all you did for me and others that made us the cooks we are today. I miss you at the family reunions; they're not the same without you.

Clarence Layton

Clarence Layton was the rue for our stew. She was my wife's grandmother. She lived a simple life and I was lucky enough to get to cook for her when she was getting on in age and to actually get compliments from her on my cooking. Unlike today, when people can come up with a number of reasons they can't make it to family functions, when Clarence Layton was doing the cooking, people came from many states to all holidays. Those days are missed by all. We do still have the Layton family reunion on her birthday in her honor, but it'll never be the same without her. I'll never forget the fried chicken she cooked, it was the best fried chicken in Gordon, Georgia or anywhere else that I've been. People showed up at family functions, who weren't even related, just to sneak a piece of it, what a compliment that was.

Recently Deborah Layton, her granddaughter, baked one of Granny's famous Caramel Cakes. My Wife wept while eating it. The emotional experience actually surpassed the taste of it because she could see her mother & Granny in the room, while she ate it. I t didn't hurt that the cake was great.

I'll never forget when my wife was driving a race car we'd built and we went by the nursing home that Granny had been staying in with it. She could no longer speak and had a board designed to spell out what she had to say. She insisted that she be taken out to the parking lot in a wheel chair. As my wife climbed into the car and fired it off on the trailer (it was quite loud as you can imagine), Granny sat in that chair with a huge smile and cried tears of joy, seeing my wife's mother's name, who was already gone, painted down the whole side of the car. It was a moment that my wife has never forgotten to this day.

Granny Layton is in every meal that I make and I'm mighty glad she's there. Her tradition has carried on in the Layton women of today and I salute them all.

KENNESAWTAYLOR

Patricia Layton Green

Patsy Green was simply the best cook I've ever known and she influenced me in ways that I'm still discovering. Recently, my wife's Dad gave her all of Patsy Green's recipes and there are many. I use them in reverence; every meal is a subtle reminder of just how much love she put into what she cooked. She raised six kids in Gordon, Georgia and I assure you when they say she was the best cooker ever, they're not stretching the truth.

I can only imagine that love had to have been one of the ingredients in most of her recipes, because I cannot duplicate them. Oh, people rave about the things I cook, but most of them never had them cooked by the master.

She had every cooking appliance or unusual spice known to man. I swear if a recipe called for eye of a falcon born on the south slop of the Andes, she would have it on one of her lazy Susan's somewhere. Every meal she cooked was amazing and I learned much from her, not the least important was how to make a thing look good, as well as taste good. Her meals had to be perfect in every way before they hit the table. Family from out of state actually had to take pictures of her table before the eating began. She could eat at a restaurant and then come back home and duplicate any meal she'd particularly liked. She could cook anything you had ever had and do a great job, simply from your description of it.

I was much honored to spend almost every day with Patsy Green during the last year of her life and will never forget that I got to cook for her for most of that year. She and Granny had lunch together once a week or so, and I was the cook. It might have intimidated others, but was simply one of the joys of my life. Patsy Green didn't invent anything that will insure her name is never forgotten. She didn't start some huge charity that will live on forever. Still, she was one of my heroes, as well as a hero to many others, because of her kindness that far surpassed what was called for.

So this year, as the dirty dishes pile up on the counter, as the flour gets into your hair while you frantically try to make sure everything gets done at the same time and is all warm, remember all those redneck cookers that make up the cook that you are. During the prayer give thanks to all those women who are a part of the cook that you have become. As you push away from the table and the compliments start to flow, make sure that they get some of the credit they deserve. These women were never famous, they didn't change history. However, they did leave a legacy that is felt and tasted in an ever growing number of tables and families each and every year.

Finally, this is an excerpt from a cookbook I'm writing called, The Redneck Cooker. Merry Christmas to all and a Happy New Year.

What Percle Said

Percle Arthur was my Grandpaw. He could say anything and make it sound grumpy, easily. On those rare occasions I spent the night at his house, he would open the bedroom door at four am and say, "Get out of bed you're gonna sleep your whole life away." I always did, I was a little scared of him. Not only was I scared of that grumpy, old man, but I had the general idea that he was about as smart as most his age, which is to say not very. I don't remember the exact quote made by Mark Twain years ago, but like him I was amazed at how smart the old guy had gotten by the time I was grown. How fortunate I feel to have become close friends with him as I grew and before he died.

On another occasion he told me he would never pay for water, dirt or air. I can only imagine what he would think, now that bottled water costs more than gasoline, there are signs everywhere that say dirt for sale and it costs seventy five cents to put air in your tires.

Another of his jewels, "If you throw enough s%t on the wall, something will stick." That has become a way of life for me and its wisdom is timeless. I could never have survived in a small business for years without this small tid bit of information. It has also served me well in my writing. You keep putting it out there and sooner or later someone likes something you've written.

The best one though, the one that really sticks out, "As soon as you realize you're dealing with an idiot, just shut up. If you argue with an idiot, you'll only upset yourself and when it's done, you'll be all upset and he'll still be an idiot." He finished this one with, "If you find them stupid, leave them stupid."

More wise words I've never heard. It has kept me out of many arguments with idiots over the years and since idiots are quick to fight, I dare to say it's kept me out of a few fights as well.

I only bring all this up because someone else said something to me recently that proves that there are still pearls of wisdom out there if you're paying attention. I don't know who actually deserves the credit for this one, but I heard it from Henry Nelson, a local Wilkinson County resident, "You can outsmart the smart, but the ignorant will defeat you." Thanks Henry, I've noticed how true this is at least two times a day since hearing it. If any of you doubt it, you've never driven in Milledgeville.

My Grandpaw said many things to me in my lifetime and I'm not too sure I paid enough attention to most of it. If I had it to do over again, I'd listen to every little piece of wisdom he imparted to me and I suggest that if you're lucky enough to still have yours, that you make it a point to see him as soon as possible.

If you're young he'll seem almost too dumb to be in the room with, but listen carefully, he knows what you're going through and where you're going to. He is the man, if you're lucky, that you will become. He is the man who can help you navigate through the impending tough times we are all facing in the immediate future.

So thank you Percle Arthur for all the wisdom you gave so freely and all the times you said things I didn't like, but things I needed to hear.

Tex

We've all known a Tex and I met two in the Navy. "Just call me Tex." You could hear his voice get lower when he said it to me. It turns out that's what he said to everyone. He was right out of boot camp, tall, skinny, blond headed, good looking and trying to act tough. He wasn't doing a good job.

A week after he came onboard, I entered the fire room just after lunch and was surprised to hear an air chipper going already. I was on the third level and all the floors are made of grating. I looked down to see him in the bilges, three floors below, chipping paint. He had on ear muffs and goggles because chippers are very loud. He would chip for a while then he'd beat the ship with the chipper. That was why he was tearing up so many of them. I'd crawled his butt several times, hard, but decided this time to cut him some slack. If you ride them too hard at first, they never become productive.

I started to go about my business, but suddenly I had a brilliant idea. I walked over to the water fountain, filled my mouth with water, then stepped up to the rail over looking him, unzipped my pants, pulled myself out and spit the water on him from three stories up. When he turned to look up I shook myself off and zipped up my pants. Now you had to be there, but let me tell you, his eyes got as big as saucers. The goggles made them look even bigger; on top of that he had those big Mickey Mouse ear muffs on.

The realization of what he thought just happened was coming on hard. He stood up unhooking the air from his chipper. I started to laugh and then got choked and feared I would lose my lunch. I was just trying to survive choking and laughing, soon tears started to run down my face. I couldn't get myself together and by the time I quite choking he was on the top flight of stairs. He was crazy with fury and had taken the stairs three at a time, tearing off his earmuffs and goggles as he came up. Still laughing pretty hard, I realized he was madder than I'd expected him to be.

He screamed, "Nobody pees on a man from Texas and lives." By the time he got to the third floor he was red in the face and you could see the veins popping from his neck. I really wanted to let him in on the joke, but couldn't get control of my laughter. I could tell, he didn't think it was funny. The madder he got the more I laughed and the less my chances were of stopping this. Then it got even more serious, he started swinging the chipper at me, which is about like swinging a heavy hammer. If he connected, I was going to the hospital, but I still couldn't tell him and couldn't protect myself. All I could do was evade his swings.

There we were, he was trying to kill me, hitting pipes while he's swinging and me dodging and laughing. I knew I couldn't last much longer. I was laughing so hard I was crying and he was getting closer with every attempt. I could have easily hit him and put a stop to it, but he hadn't really done anything to deserve it. I'd played a practical joke and it had backfired on me. He had every right to be mad.

In the middle of this a Chief came down the stairs. Having no clue what was going on and it not looking good, the Chief started yelling. Tex stopped and popped to attention, you could tell he was green. The Chief continued yelling about assaulting a senior office and how serious a crime it was.

Tex tried to defend himself, but every time he opened his mouth the Chief got louder. Tex was on the verge of tears and was shaking all over from the exertion of trying to kill me in 120 degree heat. He was sweating like a pig and looked like he was about to be sick. The Chief told him not to move and took me down to the control booth on the next floor to find out what was happening. I told the story and we laughed for about 30 minutes, almost forgetting about Tex out in the heat. When we got control of ourselves we went back upstairs.

He made him run in place, do push ups and other exercises until he threw up from the heat and exertion. The whole time Tex was probably imagining what kind of lie I'd told him. That night I had to report to the Chief's mess and do a kind of stand up comedy routine for all of the Chiefs, first classes and officers on the boat. It was the talk of the boat the next morning and although he found out the truth, he never forgot or forgave me. When I left the boat three years later, he was still called Piddle-N-Poo instead of Tex.

Wisdom Comes with Age

"When I was a boy of fourteen, my father was so ignorant I could hardly stand to have the old man around. But when I got to be twenty-one, I was astonished at how much the old man had learned in seven years." Mark Twain, Readers Digest, 1937.

I've had many jobs over the years to support my writing. Somehow, years ago, I thought it was supposed to be the other way around. Anyway, I worked as a manager at a repair shop for a while once. I met Melba there. She drove up one day in a perfect, 1970, blue Cadillac. The car looked like it was just off the showroom floor inside and out. We did an oil change, rotated and balanced the tires, admired the car a little, too long and then sent her on her way.

I was doing something else, but noticed her pull up and get out, looking at her tires, then she got back in to back up slightly. She did this several times and walked back into the waiting room. The receptionist called me to the office. Melba was maybe 5 feet tall, with short gray hair and a cane that looked as good as the car did. She was small and slightly stooped over. From her paperwork we'd learned she was 85.

"I'm very disappointed with the service here, young man and I'll tell everyone I know." She was making quite a scene in the waiting room and shaking her cane in my direction, menacingly.

I got her to go outside in an effort to defuse the situation. "What seems to be the problem?" I asked.

With her cane she pointed at her front tire, the valve stem was at the bottom. "You see that stem? It's in the right spot, the rest are wrong." We walked around the car, and sure enough, the others were in different places. I tried not to smile at the absurdity of this, out of respect.

"Mrs. Tollison, that doesn't matter at all. In fact, by the time you get home they'll have moved on to other places."

"Not so, young man. This was my Edgar's car and he said it would ride better if they were all in the right spot."

Rather than argue, I had one of the mechanics put the car back on the rack and place all the valve stems pointing down.

"You have a good day Mrs. Tollison, but I assure you when we see this car again, those stems will have migrated around."

We watched when she almost caused a wreck crossing the busy highway, then moved across the parking lot of the mall on the other side, pulled out the other end of the parking lot and returned to our shop. All business was suspended while we indulged her. When she stopped in front of us, those stems were exactly in the same spots.

"You really didn't drive far enough and you made very few turns."

"You try."

We got in and I drove around for several miles, turning one way and then the other until I was confident there would be a change. We pulled back up at the shop to all the mechanics, the receptionist and a waiting room full of people, who were all interested in our little debate. One of the mechanics waved me forward until the valve stem of the left front tire was on the bottom. We got out and twenty people walked around the car, scratching their heads and rubbing their chins. The stems hadn't moved.

Melba was quit pleased and became a fixture, stopping every time she passed by to further prove she was right. She always was. It took her a long time to put enough miles on that car to need another oil change, but months later, it did happen. When she showed up, she parked out front and made sure we all saw the stems in the same spot, before she let us move the car inside. The stems were still perfectly aligned after 4000 miles. We got very fond of Melba. She continued to stop by. We even gave her a chrome, valve stem mounted on a plaque for Christmas. We were quite sad when she died, not long after proving to an entire shop, that an old woman still knew a thing or two.

SMALL TOWNS

The Wilkinson County Redneck Cooker

On Thanksgiving we give thanks for all that we have been blessed with, not just in the last year, but in our lifetimes. There are always many more things to give thanks for than we can remember at the time. We push away from our tables stuffed with all the delicacies of the season, fat and sassy. Christmas time is a time to give thanks for all that Jesus did for us some two thousand years ago and sometimes even then, we only see the commercial side of it.

Food is a memory stimulator. It instantly transports us back to days of our youth when we eat some of the dishes we enjoyed as a child. I think that's what all the traditional food is about. Everybody sits around and watches football or plays with the kids as the smell of heavenly food permeates the house while it cooks. The cooking can go on for days and will include dishes never seen during the rest of the year. Pistachio pudding, plum pudding, even turkey and stuffing rarely make an appearance during the rest of the year.

I'm a Redneck cooker, this came about simply because I'm a redneck and when my son was about four, after a meal he said, "Daddy you're a good cooker." It's one of the best compliments I've ever gotten. That's really not how it came to be though, is it? I fuss and muss for days in the kitchen during the holidays and it wasn't always as easy and enjoyable as it is today. It used to be stressful and the pressure was on when I was younger to produce a meal that could hold a candle to those who came before. After many years, I've realized it can't be done and have relaxed to a degree.

Thinking back to all the holiday meals I've prepared, or attended, I can't remember one where all the great cooks of the past haven't been mentioned in the prayer. Maybe not thanked for their contribution to the meal, but at least mentioned out of love. After the meal, as everyone sits around and pays you compliments, you smile and bask in the success of throwing another grand meal together for your family and the warm and fuzzy feeling you get for having done it. By the way, Thanksgiving was at my house and for Christmas, I will cook at my mother's house in her kitchen.

Male cooks are especially bad about strutting around and enjoying the reputation of being a good cook and some of us deserve it, because we really are. Cooking was a way to impress the women when we were young. I wonder if my grandmother would have divulged her secrets to me if she'd known why I wanted them?

They say that behind every good man there is a good woman. I'm here to tell you that behind every good cooker, there are several, maybe even generations of good women. This is not about the women who are still with us, but the ones that are long gone. My mother, wife and sister-in-law, Leesa Green deserve a lot of credit to the contributions they have made and continue to make to this day. This is about those whose voices and love is felt, if not heard, in the smell of the turkey or the moistness of the stuffing. This is about the one you can't help thinking about when you bite into that macaroni and cheese or the fried cornbread you put on the table.

Every redneck cooker, male or female, has a long line of cookers that made them into what they are and this is the thanks for some of mine.

KENNESAWTAYLOR

Paw Paw's Poopie Head

Ok, it's official, I'm old, but somehow I feel younger than ever. Just maybe it has something to do with Michael Douglas Taylor, my first grandchild. Just like my animals, I'm quickly coming up with all kinds of silly little names for him. Poopie Head is one and I hope it doesn't stick. A friend of mine, Mike Weaver, told me to call everything he likes Paw Paw and those would be the first words he'd say. I call his mother and his granny Paw Paw every time I'm around him. Right now they think it's funny, but they won't when the first words out of his mouth are Paw Paw. I've always thought Paw Paw was a little stupid, so why do I now think it's the most beautiful phrase on the planet, hummm?

I remember when I was young and all I really had to worry about was how to come up with the gas money to cruise on Friday night and the money to buy that ever important fast food burger while doing it. Then I started dating, suddenly it was two burgers, the pressure was building. Then I met my wife, thank you God, once she moved in there were two checks coming into the house and for a brief moment things seemed to get better. Then my son was born. I loved him, but suddenly there were three fast food burgers to buy and the mint couldn't make enough money for me to buy everything else he needed.

The pressure soon took over most of the fun in life as I had to become pretty serious. It seemed like I worked all the time and on top of that, he became a butthead at about 5 and got more expensive as it went. We could hardly keep up with the bills, the ball games and all the accessories that come along with raising a little Hitler. Ok, he wasn't that bad, but when we showed up at relative's houses they shut the curtains and acted like they weren't at home. He was kicked out of every daycare in Milledgeville and eventually during the third grade was banned from the Baldwin County school buses for life, no small feat. We had to arrange transportation to and from school for the rest of his life. I loved him then, I love him now. I hope that the birth of his first child on May 16th will be the thing that pushes him to new heights of adulthood.

Now about this grandchild thing, I think all through the pregnancy I was afraid I would revisit the pressure and frustration of raising a small child and all that entails. Wrong. I was nearby when he was born and was the third person to see him. I spent way too much time watching him being weighed and measured, then stood and stared at him through the glass as he did nothing. Sure I was worried for his mother, but nothing like I worried for his grandmother all those years ago. Now, instead of holding my wallet every time I get near my son and trying to limit my exposure by not going by his house too often, I look for a reason to stop by every day and just stare at my little Poopie Head. I look forward to watching his first steps and first falls. My wallet has taken to hiding from me in self defense as it's taking a beating.

I've found that none of this is important and my wallet and I are arguing over how soon I can stop by again. Forget him, he's not a Paw Paw. I've developed a new respect for his mother and new hopes for his father. I know that this will cost me, but it's not nearly as hard as his dad was and there is pleasure in it. His Granny, poor thing, will just bust into a crying fit once in a while, simply from the joy of being a Granny. It's kind of cool. So here's to all the grandparents out there: I feel ya, and welcome to this big beautiful world to Paw Paw's Poopie head.

KENNESAW TAYLOR

Gordon's Better Hometown Halloween

Last year my wife had to work on Halloween night, so I decided to go downtown and treat myself to a dinner out. I ended up on the Front Porch restaurant and had already ordered my dinner when I realized I'd parked nearby and they were blocking off the streets. It had been a particularly hectic day and I think I'd completely forgotten it was Halloween at all. I was a little flustered when I figured out I was stuck there for two hours, my computer was calling my name.

It only took a few little ghosts and goblins to change my mind and I sat there and thoroughly enjoyed the wonderment of the children as they came up those steps with the joy that only a child can express over such little treats, plastered on their faces. It gave me such a feeling of hope to know there were still some innocents left somewhere. As the years pass, people try to stamp out Halloween as it is based on a pagan holiday. Those same people have turned Christmas into the most commercial day of the year. Leave the kids alone. If you don't want to celebrate it, that's fine, but leave those of us who do alone. Our kids lose their innocence way too soon, let them hold onto it as long as possible. Squashing Halloween is about like telling kids there is no Santa, wait as long as you can.

This year I spent the night on a different porch, the porch of Clear Creek Flowers and on purpose. The people that gathered there and at all Gordon merchants were there to give joy and they did a great job. I was glad to be part of it. For two hours kids flowed up the ramp to get their little bits of joy and those giving out the candy received much more than the children did. The costumes were great and varied, some so cute they hurt your heart.

I talked to one grandmother who came from the other side of Baldwin County almost in Hancock County to bring her grandchildren to Gordon.

"We were here last year. I know it's safe, I think it's great." Mae Johnson said. As far as I could tell there was no other Gordon connection, just a safe place to bring her grandkids for a night they will never forget. Those kids will go out into the world some day and some of their fondest memories will be trick or treating in Gordon as a child.

I want to take this time to thank Better Hometown Gordon for the job they do, last year I'd never even heard of them, this year I hold great respect for them. They not only support and raise the image of our town, but they make memories that will last a lifetime. I salute all of you for a job well done. I was lucky enough to go on the cemetery tour afterwards. Again, all involved did a great job and my grandkids loved it. I felt bad for the poor kid they shot on the tombstone for not having a ticket and that scared my grandson to death because he'd lost his. He thought he was next, we laughed until we cried.

It was a misty rainy night, but all those involved stayed the course and put on a great show. It takes special people to make something in such a small town that's safe and entertaining and continue to do it year after year.

When I was a small child Carrington Woods in Milledgeville was the safe place to go trick or treating. I'm proud that Gordon is that place now. I look forward to next year and if I'm not too busy I might just be creeping around that old cemetery myself.

Redneck Party Games

I remember the first time I ever heard, hey ya'll watch this. It was in a newspaper. Some good old boy said that right before he decided to swerve off the road to hit a sign in his truck, somewhere in Kentucky. He ended up sailing off the side of the mountain road and landing in the roof of a house. Now it's become a national joke about the famous last words of a Redneck. I said those exact words just before pulling a wheelie on my motorcycle in front of a bunch of people in Milledgeville one night, a wheelie that ended badly, with a trip to the hospital.

However the stupidest thing I ever did was followed by quotes that can't be repeated here. We were having a little get together at my house. Now, just because I quit drinking all those years ago doesn't mean that all my friends did. It was getting late, so only the diehards were still hanging around. There were about fifteen of us sitting around a large coffee table playing cards. It was actually an upright piano lying face down. We lacquered the back and it made a neat, but big coffee table. Tell me that's not Redneck.

Everyone was pretty drunk, but due to the late hour had quieted down pretty good. In fact I think we had to wake a few of them when it was their time to bet. Behind me on the wall hung my black powder rifle and my powder horn. Somewhere in the middle of this late night daze a brilliant idea popped into my head. Sitting in front of me on the table was a large ashtray filled to the brim with cigarette butts. I reached back and removed the powder horn without anyone noticing. I started talking, trying to keep everyone's eyes on my face instead of what I was doing with my hands. It's not that hard when everyone else is drunk. I poured a little powder in the ashtray. Happy that I had pulled it off and due to the fact it was pretty dark, I poured a little more. I wanted there to be enough to scare them.

I was pretty happy with myself, but after a moment or so I decided I still hadn't used enough, so I poured a little more. Nobody noticed a thing. I was really going to enjoy this. Honestly, I think I poured just a couple more times, because I was amazed no one was noticing. Then came those famous last words of a redneck. "Hey ya'll watch this." I struck a match and watched as everyone's eyes twinkled in the semi darkness, then tossed it into the ashtray.

Vaaaabooom, the explosion rocked the house and rattled the windows. The ashtray split into three pieces and everything else on the table spread throughout the whole house. Cigarette butts and ashes ended up in everyone's hair and all over their faces. We never did find all the cards. No one had eyebrows or eyelashes for some time after that. The black cloud of smoke rolled through the house and forced us all outside. At first they were all too stunned to know what had happened. But outside under a street light, we got a better look at each others faces all smudged and started laughing. We stood on the sidewalk and watched the black smoke pour from the door for a while before we could go back in. We were still finding butts in strange places when we moved from that house.

My friends were still my friends, but hey ya'll watch this, became our own little joke after that. So just pray that you never hear those words when you're riding in a car with someone.

My Two Most Memorable Haircuts

I've had two memorable haircuts in my life. The first was in 1978 when I joined the military. I, wanting to hold onto my curls that reached my rear end, didn't get a haircut before I left Milledgeville. You're not too bright at 17. Arriving at boot camp I was assigned to a temporary barracks until they could come up with the 80 guys it took to make up a company. We walked around in civvies for a week and were picked on by everyone. On the first day I complained about the fact that they hadn't cut our hair and how much flack we were catching for it.

One of the Petty Officers in charge helped me out and snuck me into the barber shop. I still love this guy today. The barbers joked as one of them cut all my hair on one side of my head. They walked away laughing, I sat in the chair for three hours waiting for them to come back, they never did. I walked around for a week with no hair on one side and hair down to my hiney on the other. It's probably funny to you now and it was funny to the 10,000 people on the base that all looked the same then, but it's never been funny to me.

I learned a valuable lesson in Korea. You get in a cab and you never say hurry. In the movies they toss the guy a bill and say step on it. In Korea you toss him one and beg him to slow down. The Taxi drivers in Korea have a code all their own. Stop signs and all other forms of traffic control are merely suggestions. You should stop here, the speed limit should be 35 on this curvy mountainous road.

Now to the second most memorable haircut. I walked into the Old Time Barbershop in Milledgeville last week. I saw no Indians outside, no hitching post. No bows and arrows were evident in the shop. I sat down in Bubba's chair and told him what I wanted. There was a sign on the wall that said, never trust a bald barber. Looking around I noticed that they all had short hair. Someone made the comment about you can't have a barbershop in the south without a barber named Bubba. Bubba moved in behind me and buzzed for about 30 seconds.

Then a video named Toes came on the TV, all haircutting stopped while all the barbers and customers watched and laughed out loud. It was the funniest thing I'd ever seen. Once it was over Bubba buzzed for about another 30 seconds, he was done. I stood up and looked in the mirror. Holy Moly! I'd walked in a hippie and was walking out a Republican, well maybe not a Republican, maybe a democrat with too much starch in his drawers. I'd never get mad over a haircut and besides I was stressed when I went in and the barbers had totally taken that away. All in all it was a good experience.

It's been the joke of the day everywhere I've been for the last two weeks. I stopped by to tell them I'd write this article and it was gonna be a big joke. Again the whole shop rolled as I retold of my adventure being scalped by Indians, right in Milledgeville in broad daylight. All business came to a stop while I visited, everyone present wore a smile the whole time I was there. Not too bad for a haircut experience, after all. Not only did they encourage the article and jokingly said we get that a lot, they wrote down the name of the shop, the video we watched and all their names for me.

After some consideration I realized that I got exactly what I'd asked for, a quick short haircut. No one called me paleface, no one spoke with a forked tongue, no one even called me Kemosabie. I of all people should know to pick my words carefully. So in closing, never walk into the Old Time Barber shop and flip them a bill and say make it short, unless you just want to be an instant Republican.

KENNESAW TAYLOR

Sweet Iced Tea and Snow

I've had many jobs over the years. I was good at most of them, too. Now my biggest job is to make sure I've got time to write. There was a time when I had to have real jobs. The company I worked for sent me to Virginia for a job on a power plant during the winter once. Now I know that most of us think Virginia was the capital of the Confederacy, but I'm here to tell you, anywhere you can't get sweet tea ain't in the south.

"Sir I can bring you some raspberry tea", one waitress said at a Dennys, she was proud of it, too. I tried it once, just made me mad. So I'd take a glass of unsweetened, add a little sugar and stir until my food was cold and it was just unsweetened tea with a bunch of sugar in the bottom. You just don't understand what it's like without sweet tea, until you don't have it. I know after so many years of joking about it, the people up north know what grits are, but you still get a laugh every time you ask about them. Don't they have corn up there? Is that all the war was about? To make sure the people up north weren't allowed to eat grits, well it worked. They won, but they still don't get to eat grits, poor slobs. If we'd have won we'd be eating, well, uh, shoot they must have some dish that is as good as grits. Ok, I guess they don't, but you get the point.

So we get there and check into our Motel, the next morning there was two feet of snow on the ground. We went to a diner and had breakfast with no tea or grits, not a good start of the day. Once we arrived at the job, we were surprised to see hundreds of people actually show up. Around here if they talk about snow, people start having wrecks in anticipation. I think they don't really want to have a wreck in bad weather, so they get it over with before the snow actually falls. Who says people in the south aren't forward thinking people?

You can't find a loaf of bread or milk at the grocery store and when it starts to fall, every one in the state gets on the road for a little redneck fun and all of them wreck at the same time. Lord help the weatherman who predicts snow that doesn't come. He's liable to find himself at the end of a shotgun barrel with a redneck on the other end that has a milk mustache and more bread at home than he'll ever eat. "Hey little feller, you told my kids it was going to snow and it didn't. You best better be findin some. Now I've got to go to work and they've got to go to school. You ain't from around here are you boy?"

So once we were at the job, it starts to rain and it's so cold the rain is freezing where it lands. "Climb up that scaffolding and replace the little glass windows on that cooling tower." someone who's never seen a grit said. I looked up, it was 150 feet tall. "Are you crazy? It's 25 degrees and raining, I ain't climbing that. Where we're from you don't go to work or school for a week if it snows for fifteen minutes." He had no sense of humor and just pointed to the scaffolding.

Up we climbed breaking the ice from the ladder as we went. We worked all day in the freezing rain, having to stop and break away ice while we worked. At home we'd have been jumping in and out the back door tending to the grill, watching the kids and dogs play in the snow.

I'm glad all those jobs were just for a few days, because when you venture above say, North Carolina, a man learns things that he just really doesn't need to know. So the first time you order sweet tea and the waitress gets a stupid look on her face. Get in your car and drive about 10 miles south and try it again. If that don't work, keep repeating this until it does.

KENNESAW TAYLOR

THE SOAP BOX

Sailors and Singers

In September 1980 I turned twenty. I think I was in Auckland, New Zealand and was just about to finish a nine month tour overseas. I'd spent that time learning many things I never needed to know, things that many in our Country never learn. Who can say if we need to know them or not? I'd learned to drink and learned about death; both from natural causes and from the most unnatural causes you can imagine. I'd learned about starvation and what a mother will do to feed her kids.

I'd seen the greatest this earth has to offer and the worst it can produce. Truth, that's the biggest lesson a young man can learn. I learned the truth that so many never even catch a glimpse of. Small minds always stay small, so many never see out of their twenty miles of experience. I'm not saying I needed to know all this, I'm just saying I don't know how people can live with such a limited view of the world.

On December 5, 1980 we pulled into Pearl Harbor, Hawaii. There was to be a memorial service on the 7th for all the fallen sailors. I was a sharp sailor so I was picked to take place in it. On the appointed day I stood in that Memorial at attention and listened to an officer give a touching speech about the over 1000 men who died on the U.S.S. Arizona, the ship that rests below the Memorial. It is a very chilling thing for a sailor to see a sunken ship. I don't care how many you see, they still chill you to the bone. As you stand on that Memorial and look down into the water it gives you great pause to see the Arizona lying there, the stack sticking from the water, the oil drops still rising to the surface after so many years. The tears of the Arizona they are called.

I stood that day in full dress whites and cried along with everyone in attendance. Ships circled the Memorial as we performed our tasks. It was the most profound day of my life in many ways. I had just finished my year long course on life, death and what it all means in the grand scheme of things, or so I thought. After that day I went ashore to do what most sailors do, which is to get drunk in the shortest amount of time with the smallest amount of money possible. I went about my job with a little more conviction than usual and soon found myself waking up on Waikiki beach, slightly disheveled. Getting up I straightened my uniform and went back to the scene of the crime to start all over again.

The lessons of the Arizona had been hard and had caused much pain. I was dealing with them the only way I knew how. Most people know where they were when John Kennedy died. I was only four and probably never skipped a beat playing with my G.I. Joe, never even noticed. Nor did I notice when Martin Luther King died, again I was young. On December 8, 1980 I was in a bar called the Red Lion just a few blocks from Waikiki beach and I was drinking like the Olympic drinker I'd become. I stumbled out and made my way to the beach taking off my clothes as I went. I skinny dipped, drunk in the Pacific Ocean. Climbing back out I dressed and lay down alone to sleep off another night of drowning the memories of all those men on the Arizona and the others who shared their same fate. It had been a melancholy week.

Waking up on December 9th I straightened my uniform once again and made my way back to The Red Lion and ordered a beer for breakfast. It was then that Yoko Ono addressed the nation about the death of John Lennon. I sat at that bar with a room full of strangers and wept like a baby. We were suddenly family and soon the bar filled to capacity. We drank all day and listened to John Lennon songs on the radio. We shared a day that I will never forget. Everyone in the room shared addresses and swore to never forget each other or what we had shared. I never heard from a single person in that room again and they never heard from me. I'll never forget the day that John died or where I was. I'd heard American Pie by Don McLaine all my life, but had never understood it until then. I wish I didn't understand it now. Imagine all the people.

I know that some will struggle to understand what John had to do with the others mentioned here. I served proudly, all those sailors at Pearl Harbor died fighting the tyranny of a hand full that would rule the world for their own sick purposes. Martin died fighting oppression from the majority. John Kennedy died showing us all that we could make a difference. John Lennon fought his own war, a war for peace, a war that is still no less a war.

Lessons of 2009

Let me start with I've learned that Wilkinson County Post readers are some good people. This may appear to be a complaining session, but it really is just some observations. I look forward to the New Year and spending it with all of you.

As with every year, we have learned much. If you make a difference in the world you'll still be mourned when you pass. Even if you made a few mistakes along the way, Ted Kennedy and Michael Jackson taught us that. Tiger too has passed in a sense, but he'd have had to be driving a fifteen-passenger bus when he went off that bridge to get the job done. Is it just me or is one woman too much to juggle?

We've learned that you can be young charming, popular and hot, even if you're an old fogie like me. All you've got to do is get on Myspace, Facebook and Twitter all at one time. I've met several people that have been dead for 200 years, still not sure how that works. You learn that you can be seen in at least four places at one time and somehow, someone on each saw you everywhere you weren't at. You learn that no one is too old to start Facebooking, no one really cares if they can spell and what rotflmao means. Did I need to know that? I learned that one out of ten people in the Country is a writer and none of them mind telling you why you aren't one.

We were told who could and who couldn't be the President for many years. We learned this year that someone has been lying to us all our lives. We learned a singer can make it even with all the cards stacked against her, thank you Susan Boyle. You give this old crusty writer hope. Oh and one last thing about social networking, the friends you make are really friends and are nice to meet. I've met several hundred and it's been a hoot.

We learned that if you buy a house you can't afford, you can't afford it. If you buy one and lose your job it amounts to the same thing. We've learned that if you rename a virus after a pig, you can make record profits during a recession from the common cold. That will start some mess, I bet. We've learned that if you're going to give billions of dollars to the American people, just give it to the ones who've stolen the most, it seems to make sense to the ones with the most money. Save the banks and automakers, but let the ones who actually keep the Country afloat become homeless.

We've learned that the biggest heroes are often the biggest villains. Oh, who can forget that Bernard Madoff made off. Farrah proved that like a flower, even beautiful things were born to die. Patrick Swazey taught us that love is timeless. David Carradine taught us even the tough lose eventually. We found out that Humpty Dumpty was the blueprint for the stock market. Who knew? I've got to look up who wrote that, he was a forward thinker.

We've come to learn that even though the politicians are all saying the same thing, somehow they can't agree it's the same thing. Health care will cost us billions no matter whose idea it is and then all it will do is make it mandatory for people to have it, even if they can't afford it. Hey, homeless with health insurance, what a concept. I guess when they make it mandatory all artists will end up in jail and will have it for free anyway, an unexpected upside. Glad it came to me.

I guess the biggest lesson I've learned from all this is that if you get caught with your hands in the cookie jar, they'll just buy a bigger cookie jar and turn their heads while you're in the kitchen. If you get caught with your pants down as a golfer, you might as well leave em down it saves you time. If you're a football player, you better pay attention to where your girlfriend shops and what she buys or sleep with one eye open. If you're a wolf, the government has one great big hen house and all the chickens are stamped U.S.D.A.approved.

KENNESAWTAYLOR

Love in Recession

As with all things recession hits us where it hurts, at the gas pumps, on our electric bill, at the grocery store and on our insurance. I think most will agree that our retirement programs have taken a pretty hard hit, too. I've got to tell you though that until talking to a friend the other day, I had no idea just what it does to love. I think we'll stay out of calling names on this one, because after having the idea for this story, I talked to several people who added a little.

He said, the first thing I did was fall madly in love with a girl at the local convenience store. I figured she could sneak me a little gas. I found out I was wrong. Suddenly I was much less fond of her and she did have that large wart, so I broke my own heart and had to let her go. It was the best three days of my life.

With gas getting higher, my hunting grounds shrunk considerably. I knew I'd have to settle for a drunk chick with few teeth and an over protective father near home, instead of one just like her in Macon. I found love number two at the local fast food restaurant. It only took about a week for the manager to realize I was eating three meals a day there and wasn't paying for any of them. I would have stayed with her anyway, but they fired her for it and well I just need someone who isn't too lazy to work, so once again I had to deal with the loss of the love of my life.

I went to the bank looking for my next love, but every time one smiled at me she had all her teeth and dressed better than I did. I was out of my element, but I tried for a little while. My cousin, who used to work at a bank, informed me that try as you might there was just no way to steal money. That ended that vein of gold I was mining, well that and the fact that they locked me up for stalking and banned me from the bank forever. I think I'm gonna look it up in the dictionary, cause I still ain't too sure what corn has to do with love.

Then I had a stroke of brilliance. I dressed in my best clothes and went to the local manufacturing plant, just as the whistle was blowing. Hey lots of girls, maybe I'd get one who didn't have a ride or her husband was just late picking her up. I pulled up and opened the passenger side door and stood there as hundreds of women came out. After they were all gone I noticed seven other guys doing the same thing and one of them was wearing a bow tie. We looked at each other shrugged our shoulders and left. Still I tried it for a few days until they closed the plant and moved it to Mexico. I thought about it, but I decided the girls down there just don't make enough money and I can't learn to say cervesa, which is just a Mexican way to say beer.

I tried the college women, but realized after the first day on campus that the police have no sense of humor and they really weren't capable of having an intelligent conversation with a man with a third grade education. It's a shame too, they were real pretty.

So I sat around the house for a few weeks until my savings and retirement ran out. Which means I sold the rusty 57-ford truck and the three old Camaro's I had in the front yard. I still got a Rambler and an Oldsmobile in the back yard, but I figure a man can only let himself go so far.

Then it happened. I noticed the girl that lives across the road about two doors down from me. I'd noticed her before, in fact as a kid I would walk all the way around the block to avoid her if she was in the yard. I swear it's true love this time. She has all her teeth, her hair is almost the color it was in the beginning, her father hasn't shot at me in at least 5 years and her brother can say cervesa in case we ever go down to get locked up in Mexico. I tell ya, it's true love. I don't think I can live without her. She's got the warts, she's mean as a pole cat, but she works at Wall Mart and gets a 10 % discount. I have learned a valuable lesson, there is someone out there for all of us, even when you can't afford the gas to go look for them.

KENNESAWTAYLOR

Three Strikes and You're Out

This is my commentary on the health care plan. I've noticed that those who lobby against it the loudest are the ones that have health insurance. I lied about my age and went to work young at a textile mill and have had health insurance most of my life. With the vast wealth I've made from writing, I may never have it again.

I had an accident when I was 16 and dislocated my shoulder. I was on BCBS, sorry, that's as close to a name as you'll get. At the hospital, once they'd determined my age, they wouldn't treat me without a guardian's signature. I have no idea where my mother was, but my grandmother would have to do. She came and signed for them to put my shoulder back in place. Soon I joined the Navy and was gone. I learned a few years later that the insurance company that I'd been paying for almost three years refused to pay because my grandmother wasn't my legal guardian. The hospital sued her, causing her financial hardship and she never even told me.

Fast forward to the year I got out of the Navy. I was working for a company in Florida and again had BCBS. I dislocated my shoulder on the job once again. BCBS refused to pay again, this time saying it was a pre-existing condition. Yeah, one they didn't pay for the first time. Luckily all I had to pay was the deductibles since workman's comp paid the rest.

As all good things, they come in three's. In 1985 I was working for a plant in Eatonton and dislocated it again while at home. The doctor said, "Well shoot, he's got insurance. Let's do a little surgery that'll keep this from happening again." The surgery was done and it cost tons of money. I couldn't work for two months and you guessed it,

BCBS refused to pay again because it was a pre-existing condition. Three times to the plate and three time BCBS failed to make a hit. This one forced me into financial ruin.

I'm not saying that we need a government run health plan, but it seems we need some kind of control on the insurance companies that rule the medical system. Seeing how I write a little, I get approached by many people all the time wanting to complain about the issues. Here's what I've been hearing.

The people that are against government run health care keep calling it socialized medicine. I'm not sure that's a good word to use for it. The rest of the free world went to this many years ago. How is it that in this, the most enlightened Country in the world, a Country with the best medical system, that we deny that care to the masses? One of the arguments I hear the most is that those other Countries, Canada for instance, has such a bad system that people cross the border to come here for treatment and surgery. That argument stinks, considering that those who do this have the money to go wherever they want to get the best care. Even Americans, who have the money, go to other Countries to get treatment that we won't approve.

So those of us who have insurance are so concerned about our own needs that we would deny the multitudes rudimentary coverage because we fear our coverage will suffer. At least in those other Countries all citizens have some type of coverage and have the chance to live full lives and not to be ruined in our old age by the illnesses that will eventually overtake us all. So many think that this doesn't affect them, the number of people without insurance grows every day. The economy has placed many who've never been without it in a place they've always been too good to go to. People are homeless who had everything just a few months ago. The system is broken and I don't know the answer, but we need to work together as a nation to find it. The time for partisan politics is long passed, but someone forgot to tell the people with the money and power.

The system as it is causes too much strain on the hospitals due to bad debt. It causes way too much trouble for the doctors due to malpractice litigation. It causes financial ruin for many citizens whose only crime is having an accident. It causes so many of our older citizens to die heavily in debt due to whatever disease eventually kills them. We are all paying every day for the uninsured of this Country. If those who are on a soapbox knew the real numbers, they'd know that it will cost us less to have a medical system that takes care of everyone than it does for the one we have now.

The political system continues to try to drive a wedge between the American people. They try to make us believe that we are so different. In fact we think more alike than different. Right now the plan presented by both sides is basically the same; just a matter of language separates the two. If you believe what is said by both sides you'd move to Cuba. Disinformation and idiocy prevail in this money/vote driven system. I love this Country and am damn tired of all the rhetoric we have to endure on a daily basis and it's way past time to do something about it.

College Education

I worked at a college for several years in the maintenance department. I maintained the boilers that provided the heat and electricity for the students. Every Monday, if I wasn't busy, I would go out and help the other guys replace every fire extinguisher and exit sign in every dorm. The students would destroy them all every weekend. By our calculations it was costing the school about three thousand dollars a week. They increased the security budget and added cameras, which cost them more and still it continued; only now the cameras were being painted and destroyed every weekend, too.

Then someone had the bright idea of leaning on doors and pushing pennies in the crack, which put so much pressure on the door that it couldn't be opened from the inside. What it also did, was destroy the door knobs. So it became someone's full time job just to repair door knobs, which was costing them another thousand dollars a week.

This was a predominately black school in another state. Before you get on your soapbox, there was another school 20 blocks away, a major school and mostly white, a friend of mine worked there and they had the same problem. Color has no part in the lack of respect of the young in our Country.

One night, as it often happened, the boilers were having some problem that needed the attention of a certain redneck whose job it was to keep them out of trouble, so my beeper went off at about 10 pm. I got dressed and went to check out the problem. I arrived to a campus filled with cars and cops. I got my radio and was reminded by security that Louis Farrakhan was speaking in the auditorium. I moved to the boiler house located in a remote corner of the campus and quickly got the boilers to stop acting up.

At about 11pm I was leaving the boiler house when the chief security officer hit me on the radio, "Stay where you are, I repeat, do not leave the building."

So I stood on the loading dock and watched from a distance while the crowd of students, so fired up by the speech of this prominent leader, spilled from the auditorium and proceeded to tear the campus apart. They set fires, busted windows and even turned over police cars. I spent the night there as the riot spilled into the surrounding neighborhood. It took the police all night to get it under control. The damage was only surpassed by the damage done the night hurricane Hugo passed through. I was there that night, too and spent the night in a gym full of scared kids, trying to keep them calm and safe.

The numbers were never released, but in our estimation, that visit cost the college about $50,000 dollars in damages. The money came from private donors so the college didn't have to report the real numbers in the papers or to the public. The whole thing was pretty much swept under the rug.

The issue is, what do we do about our school systems? What do we do about the lack of respect? We as a nation have created this problem and we must repair it. I wish I knew what the answer was. Maybe you can e-mail me with your ideas. Kids are coming out of our schools with little to no education. It's not the teachers fault; we have the most qualified teachers in the world. What is the answer?

Real Men Don't

There are some things the government ought not to do. Plucking a dumb old country boy like me out of Baldwin county and turning his butt lose on the unsuspecting populous of Asia is one of them. However they never learned and continued to do it. Now I know that you know that real men love Jesus and don't hit women, but here are a few that you might not know.

Growing up in Milledgeville I never rode in a cab. Real men can get a ride, ride a bike or walk wherever they need to go. It was just something you didn't do, add to this that the smell would usually gag you and would probably kill livestock if you let the windows down and you might get an understanding of why.

Pay close attention here, real men don't use umbrellas. A little rain never hurt any real man I've ever known. Besides you look like a girl with one in your hands. I don't mind looking like a girl mind you, but I sure hate being the ugliest one you ever saw.

When I spent a couple years overseas I found out that riding in a cab while often dangerous, was necessary. I've cowered in cabs all over the world, my only defense, drinking heavily. For example, you'll never get in a cab in Korea and flip the guy a buck and say hurry. You're more likely to flip him a buck and beg him to slow down, pay attention to where he's going or obey road signs.

You see road signs and laws are not enforced over there. Signs, lines on the road and stoplights are merely suggestions. You should stop here, you should take this dangerous mountain curve at thirty-five, three cars will not fit between the yellow line and the white line. If you've never ridden in a cab in a foreign country, well you just ain't lived and I'm not sure you have as close a relationship with God as you think you do. I've rode in Jeepneys in the Philippines that should have held ten people, with twenty-five in them. Oh yeah and in most countries whoever blows the horn first isn't at fault in the wreck. So they run the streets wide open with horns blaring everywhere, smoke belching from the tailpipes.

I'll never forget the only umbrella I ever bought. We pulled into Singapore and docked next to the biggest mall I'd ever seen, it was blocks of stores. Once we were free to leave the ship we had to go through the mall to get to the street and to the cabs that would take us to the beer, our only real goal. It was the middle of the Monsoon season. The Monsoon season goes from raining so hard that you can't even see to drive to actually raining so hard you can't see your hand in front of your face. I doubt seriously that any of you have ever seen rain so hard you can't walk in it.

About thirty of us stopped in a store and there is where we saw our first umbrella that kind of pulled down into itself, you know the compact ones. Before that we'd only seen the old long ones. We all had to have one and they were only a buck, so I bought my first umbrella. The others un-strapped theirs and started popping them open in the mall. Not me, that was bad luck. See, even dumb old country boys know a thing or two.

We exited the building and stood under an awning looking across the fifteen feet to where the cabs sat waiting. It was raining so hard that we could barely see them.

In a perfect world thirty sailors in dress whites would have mashed their little buttons and their umbrellas would have popped out in unison. All black umbrellas and all us in dress whites, great picture right? The problem is I've never lived in a perfect world. I had not un-strapped mine as the others had, so when we pushed our buttons the other twenty-nine made that cute little popping sound, mine shot off like a rocket. When it reached the end of the little chrome bar it kept going. We stood there and watched it arc out over two rows of cabs into the traffic and smack the windshield of a car. We stood there and watched a fifteen car pile up happen within twenty feet of us. You've never seen so many sailors scramble to cram into the waiting cabs so fast in all your life, umbrellas being dropped, broken and abandoned in the process. Every cab that would still run involved in the wreck or not, scrambled out into traffic horns blowing frantically.

All that was left of my umbrella was the handle I was still clutching. I stuffed it under the backseat, looking behind us nervously. It made the front page the next day. Unidentified sailor causes fifteen car pile up in front of mall. Crap, I'm glad they never figured out it was me. I was to find out later that they would cane you for about anything in Singapore. I'm glad I didn't get caned for buying a defective umbrella, it was the only one I ever bought.

Bail Out Verses Mail out

I have watched the current bail out of the banks and auto industry closely, as the rest of you have. I watched while the government gave or proposed to give 177 billion dollars to the people who started this thing in the first place. No problem, it's only ink and paper. Now I'm not the sharpest tool in the shed, but according to my math, if they'd given every man, woman and child in America one hundred thousand dollars, it would have cost us a lot less money.

Even after such a bailout, I heard on the news this morning that the banks are in trouble again and the auto industry has yet to even show signs of improvement. This is our money, not just ours, but our children and grandchildren's money. I hear people every day talk about the impending redistribution of wealth. As far as I can tell it's already happened, only they took it from us and future generations, to give to the wealthiest among us.

On the other hand if they had mailed out all Americans a hundred grand, what would have happened? I would have bought a new truck and paid off most of my bills. Many would have bought Christmas presents, new cars and generally gone on a spending spree with their new found wealth until it was gone, possibly catching up their mortgages and paying a few bills somewhere along the way. The smartest of us, which has turned out not necessarily to be true, would have invested it in the stock market or in real estate since homes are so cheap right now.

All aspects of our economy would have felt the positive impact of such a large influx of cash. It would have started at the bottom, eventually ending up in the same place, at the top. However, the trip it made through our economy on its way would have been the stuff of history. It would have saved many honest people, who through no fault of their own find themselves in dire straights. It would have placed money in the coffers of the banks and the auto industry that was earned, not handed to them. The major difference is that the average person would no longer be losing their home. The retailers would have had the best retail season ever, creating many jobs and producing new orders for factories all over the world. Lord, don't get me started on that.

I guess, given the state of our government, that one could not expect them to do something so simple that might actually work. I guess it made sense to take billions and give it straight to the top people in the Country, totally bypassing the rest of us. I think if I was you, I'd write a letter to my Congressman and ask them where my hundred grand was. I'm going to write a little ditty about it and submit it too my local paper. If enough of us did something, maybe we could get something done. After all, we keep hearing we have the power.

Maybe it's too late. Much of the money had been distributed already and has made little difference according to all reports. In fact soon we will be watching again as the government debates its next move, a move that will ultimately cost you and me much more in the long run. Even if someone decided this was a route worth taking, they would realize that the presses can't print money as fast as they can give it away. Unfortunately, they'll realize this after they've bailed out the richest in the Country and before they mailed out the hundred grand to the rest of us.

Maybe the question is: Where is my hundred grand? Maybe it's: Where is your hundred grand? Either way, ask your Congressman.

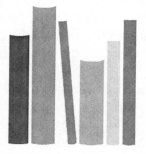

KENNESAW TAYLOR

THE ARTS

Life is not Beauty

A painting, a song, a perfect set of sentences strung together to make a story that stands the test of time. Something that says a thing so well, it resonates backward and forward in time, eternity in a paragraph. Rare are the colors, the melody, the words, art when it happens, beauty when it's right.

Art is only a reflection of life formed to give one a glimpse of what life has the potential to be. Created to ease the suffering of the masses, to give hope and meaning to the family of man. Who knows from what dark secret corner of the mind it does flow?

Art is not life, beauty can not conquer reality, they exist and struggle to compensate for life's horrors. The world moves on, starvation gains ground, genocide is carried out. Hitler lived, Jim Jones died taking many with him. Women, children and the world are raped and abused as the artist paints a better painting. The elderly die forgotten and lonely as the writer writes his love. The sick and dying of the world are doing so with a song on their lips.

Writing is a sacrifice to your soul. Rare is the success that gains fame or fortune. Maybe success is merely that one sentence that changes the world for the briefest of moments. Those moments may come only after the artist is long dead. The chance is worth the price. Where does the artist pay? When does he pay? He pays a little every time he sees the truth hidden in plain view, every time he pulls a small piece of beauty from that truth, a piece of beauty that he sees even as the ugliness and inconsistencies of life continues to prevail.

Art is not life, but life is hidden deep within it. Life is not art, but we few, must strive to forge the two, to hide the horror, to sooth the soul of man. Death is our destiny, to smile is our dream, peace is our hope, but life, life is our reality. Art fights on with little chance of winning, but it's the fight that counts.

KENNESAW TAYLOR

Small Newspapers

I doubt that this makes it to the paper, but I must write it. I wonder if all the readers out there understand the importance of the local newspapers or just how hard it is for the few staff members they can afford, to get it put together every week. I'm not talking about me, I just write a fluff article every week. In fact my dogs and cats write some of them and I just get the credit.

I'm talking about the nuts and bolts of the community, the things you need to know. Who's been born and who's died. What school is doing well and what programs aren't working. What plants are laying off people and what may be on the horizon that'll make it better. I've gotten to know several editors and their assistants over the last year and my respect for them has grown considerably.

You would think that a once a week paper is not much of a deadline. You'd be wrong. Think of all the research that it takes to write just one story. Think of all the time that it takes to put the paper together in time for it to go to print. Selling advertisements and then getting them in the paper. Local papers are going out of business at an alarming rate. The younger generation doesn't read as much as the older one does. Many simply don't care what's going on around them. You need to start caring, it's your kid's schools, it's your healthcare system and it's your County systems that are being discussed.

Think about the overwhelming number of calls, e-mails and letters the paper receives every week. I'm here to tell you that small newspapers are the backbone of our Country and I'm here to give a shout out to those who keep them going. Thank you Donna and Amanda, at the Wilkinson County Post, thank you Pam and Chris, at the Baldwin Bulletin and thank you to all the countless others who struggle for us, all over the Country every week.

KENNESAWTAYLOR

The Cliff

Before we start this thing, please realize I'm a pretty conservative guy. I'm not trying to get you to stray from the tried and true way of doing things. Plan for your future, it's important. With that said, here I go, hold on it might get a little bumpy.

If you never jump from the cliff, you never know if you can fly. If no one ever jumped, we'd have no cars, trains or airplanes. We'd have no Mozart's, no Garth Brooks, no Beatles. We'd have no Van Gogh, no Michael Angelo, no Frank Lloyd Wright. We'd have no land of the free, because those old boys jumped off the biggest cliff ever when they signed the Declaration of Independence.

We'd have no Socrates, Aristotle, Lewis Grizzard. Imagine that and no me. Ok, I crossed a line, but that's the fun of being me. I don't have a clue where the line is. We'd never have sailed the seas or touched the moon. We'd never have met George or Beetle Bailey, any of the characters of the Wizard of Oz or Beaver Clever.

Ok, you get the idea, what a small boring world it would be if no one ever took a leap of faith. I've watched all my life as people stood on the precipice and peered into the unknown and never took that first step, artists, musicians and writers who were brilliant, but afraid, people who were so wrapped up in day to day survival that taking a little risk just seemed an over the top idea.

John Paul Jones said, "He who will not risk, cannot win." So go about your daily lives and take care of what you need to for your future. Always dream, never stop thinking about what is in you that will change the world. When you've done all you must do, take just a little time to live the stuff of your dreams out loud. You may be the next Frank Sinatra, John Wayne, Martin Luther King or John Kennedy. Imagine the world without their leaps.

I've never had this problem. I've stood on that cliff many times. I look for a moment, get a running start and jump as hard and high as I can. Most times I end up in a pile on the rocks far below, but each time I learn a little itty bitty lesson about flying. Each time the view from above lasts longer and it's amazing. I'll keep on jumping until one day I glide gracefully along, enjoying the view that few ever see. I've heard it said that each of us have the option to write our own lives, but most leave it to someone else to do it. Live your dreams, dream your lives.

Painting Love

I've been asked how a man can write about love. In fact I've been asked this question many times in the last month. I think that it's wrong to assume only women can write about love, so here's my answer.

No one writes about love, they paint it in words. They take out their palate, their brushes and all the colors of the rainbow and then they bare their heart. That first love comes out in earthy shades and as it pours from the heart it flows through the brush to paint the shadowy outline of that woman you'll never live without again on the canvas. To paint love in its truest form, one must have known love.

The first time you held hands with someone comes forth, too. The joy that ran from your fingers to your heart, that joy is still there stored safely where it should be. When you choose to paint love it flows through those fingers again to add shape and depth to the painting that is what your life is about, what it will always be about.

That first kiss, the one you'll never forget, it brings in the features of the face of the beauty you strive to create. The supple lips, slightly turned up nose and the things that were important on that day of days. Then the first time you really felt love that you knew you'd die without, that's when the eyes captivated you and you knew you'd just seen your fate. That's where the painting really starts to take its shape. The eyes I think are what really sets your heart and brush on fire.

Ah, but what good is the perfect face without the smooth silky hair that wraps up the package so neatly. That hair that's always in her way, but for some reason is never in yours. You paint on like a fiend and details start to flow. You give her everything you seek, everything you've always had. The line of her neck that shows, it's something you never forget. You've traced it so many times awake and as you sleep. A silhouette as she stood in front of a curtain years ago during a full moon, another painting perhaps, another story lurking deep inside.

The laugh that you can hear even in a crowd, it shows in the brush's strokes. The smell she leaves behind as she leaves a room. I'm not talking about the smell of any perfume. The sounds of her as she sleeps, so soft and comforting, the smell she leaves on the bed sheets. Have you ever just smelled her side of the bed in the middle of the day for no reason? I have, try it, it adds another dimension to your painting.

All these things come together with great sweeps of the hand. Dip the paint, mix the colors and invent a few more. Paint the painting of your life, the painting of your love. Figure out how to paint the breath you take, the beating of your heart and you my friend have found the place to start. Your mind has millions and millions of thoughts each day. I bet you'd be surprised how many are simply about her face. How many of them make you smile and are so fleeting you can never catch them.

The touch that comes so slightly, just when you need it, when all seems to be so gray. The lips that press your cheek so lightly each morning and then throughout the day. Now this isn't supposed to be a poem, knock it off Kennesaw.

So how do you write love? You pull out your heart, you pick up your pen or brush. You dip them into the contents of your heart and you start. Your very life's blood mixes with the paints and pens. You write about all the past loves you've known, each one special in it's own way. If it works, if you pull it off, your heart is on the page for all to see.

So for me the question makes very little sense. If I could ask one back of you, I'd really appreciate it. E-mail me at <u>kennesawt@gmail.com</u> and give me your answers. How could anyone who has ever known love, not write, paint, sculpt or sing of it each day?

KENNESAWTAYLOR

Rural Writer One

You really start to tell your age when you admit that you remember when your address started with rural route one. Back when you could place a letter in the mailbox with actual money and the mailman would put a stamp on it and even leave you change. Back when penny candy was a penny and a stamp wasn't much more. I spend about fifteen dollars a week on postage now.

I wanted to give a little insight into what it takes to be a writer in a rural area. I get up at five A.M. every morning and write like a fiend for four hours. My two fingers fly across the keyboard quickly, if not gracefully, as I gulp coffee. I'm working on incorporating a third finger into the mix, but it acts like it's in a union and thus far resists my efforts.

I get up and go out into the world and make a living, being a handy man of sorts. I find myself doing things that defy rational behavior sometimes, because people in the country have a different outlook on what needs to be done. I find that some of the strangest requests are made by the most interesting people. I have to find a way to make a living and continue to provide the mail people with the kind of lifestyle they're accustomed to, something my writing has yet to become aware of, by the way. If you see it, whisper a little something in its ear. Will ya?

I work a part time job that keeps me up most of the night on Tuesdays and makes me work every Saturday, plus I do the cooking at my house. Now I've started a writers club that will take up one evening a month. You better love any artistic endeavor you start, because it is work and it does take time.

Add to this that my wife is kind of the crazy, cat lady, only she has cats, dogs and birds. So wherever I'm at or whatever I'm doing, I must stop at lunch and make my way home to leisurely stroll around the block with our dogs. They love it, but they're not trying to make a living. It may be the highlight of their day and I guess that makes it OK.

On top of that a family of cats had taken up residence where my wife works and for some reason they have to eat at ten thirty A.M. sharp. I don't know who set up their schedule, but I need to have a word with them. So on the days that my wife's schedule doesn't conform to the cats, usually two or three days a week, I stop and go feed the cats at the appointed time.

I've looked up writer in the dictionary and none of this is there. My office is small, but I share it with the cat's litter box and their food. Not the cats at work, but the three at home. As I write this, one is using the facilities, one is eating and the other is trying to knock things off my desk. I guess that's Ok, that's why I have those other eight fingers. One of my dogs is under my desk looking up at me while the other is lying under my chair. Neither fits where they are, but I don't have the heart to break it to them. If I don't cover the keyboard when I go after a fresh cup of coffee, one of the cats will have gotten to it and written several sentences before I return. Sometimes it's better than what I've written.

So when people ask what I do, I always say I'm a writer and they probably have this idea that a writer sits around all day pecking away expertly at the keyboard, sipping coffee. Not in my world, in my world a writer is a dumb, old country boy who has something to say, but has much more to do.

So if you're thinking about following your dreams and starting on the pursuit of some artistic journey, remember that it took oil for the Clampet's to get out of Bugtussle. So I've been sitting down and looking for oil in my computer for years, but at this point it looks like I may be a rural writer for a long time to come.

KENNESAWTAYLOR

A Successful Writer

How do you tell if you're a successful writer? I know, I know, ask me. As life has moved on, I've always wanted to be a writer. Visions of piles of money 12 feet high and a nice little office with a view have always dominated this dream. Strolling around New York drifting from one party to the other, dressed in some outlandish clothing with an entourage has been part of the vision, too. While I'm dreaming, having a book or two on the bestsellers list isn't too bad either. Being this decade's version of Lewis Grizzard, hey I'll take that.

Now let's talk about the reality of being a successful writer. If you're lucky, you'll have a few hours a week that you have the time to do it. If you're really lucky, you'll have a person who actually believes you can write. If you're extremely lucky, you'll have a few people who'll give you odd jobs that pay the bills while you do it. There is no way to work a full time job and write with all your heart. Ok, well in my case, it's with the two brain cells I've been able to hold on to over the years. Still every once in a while, they decide to dance together and the results are amazing.

A successful writer must have many talents. He must be able to run a cash register, sweep and mop floors with precision, cook well enough to keep his support happy and be able to build anything. He must also be able to survive on minimum sleep and the joy that a good story gives. He must have skin as thick as that of an elephant and determination beyond that of the normal person. One thing is for sure, he can't be normal. Hey, that's one thing I'm good at.

He must be selling and pushing his writing, even in his sleep. He must talk to many people every week to expand his audience without driving people crazy. Oops, too late. It's tough hammering people as much as possible without turning them off. I'm currently juggling about 14 papers, which are slowly paying attention. I'm working on a publisher and an agent at the same time, sometimes more than one. I'm dealing with 10 stores that have my book and book signings that steal much of my writing time.

My butt hurts because the money that writing produces won't even pad my seat, much less get 12 feet tall. In fact I spend three times as much on my writing as it makes.

I worry about nuclear war, but someone sitting on my glasses would be an international incident in my house. My computer crashing would be worse than the swine flu in my world. Running out of odd jobs to do, having to get a full time job and do all this at the same time would be unimaginable. I tell others all the time, most artists die hungry and I'm practicing for that. I have several family members and friends that support what I do to the end. I have as many who want to know when I'll forget all this foolishness and get serious. I'm sure that has been asked of all the other artists throughout history. That must be at least one of the qualifications of being a writer, hey one more down.

In school and in all the books I've read, there are many things that make a writer successful. You must know how to spell, your grammar must be unquestionable and you must understand the elements that make up a story. You must have a good imagination and the talent to make use of it. Practice, you must have tons of it. A good sense of humor never hurts. Above all that, beyond all that, you must have the will of a bulldog. You must live to write and write to live. Once started, you can no more stop writing than breathing. You must be a tireless self promoter, even while you turn from one closed door to the other.

Sometimes you must simply be just ignorant and innocent enough to believe you can make it against all odds, two qualities I happen to have in abundance. What does it take to be a writer? One of my friends said you have to be dead to be a successful artist, holy moly, not encouraging words. So I guess in the future, I'll find a physic and let the rest of you in on what it took to be a successful writer. Until then I'll keep punching away at my keyboard in hopes that somebody, somewhere, someday likes something I write, oh and has some money.

The Slightest Touch

As we struggle through this life, we find a select handful of people that slightly touch us in some way. The touch reverberates long after they're gone. As I get older, I've had a glimpse of how I've touched others; some of them have come to me to let me know. Each time it's been something that seemed so small to me, but was a big deal to them at the time. I too have had those who touched me in some small way that has affected me throughout my life. I find that the older I get, the more important it is to communicate this to them.

Sometime in the 9th grade, someone had the good sense to put me in a career based class at Boddie Middle School. As I was working full time, had only recently witnessed the killing of my step-father and was trying to help raise my younger sisters, the possibility of my making it through school was slim. Here is where I met Ms. Marian Bush. She did her job, teaching me how to fill out applications and how to go on job interviews, but she did much more than that. I submitted an essay to her; one sentence, four pages long, and proudly announced to her that I'd be a writer someday. I could see the pain in her face while she struggled to explain to me that it was not only bad, which it was, but that I'd never be a writer, which I may never be. She told me that if I wanted to be a writer, it would take years of work. I've still got that story and it has to be some of the worst writing ever.

Only recently, after meeting her as an adult, did I learn she told me this in the first 2 years of her career which spanned 30 years in the Baldwin County school system. I was disheartened and didn't jump out and become a writer the next day; but it struck me, I could never have had handled this as well as she did. Still as the years slipped away, I found myself writing more and more. I read everything about writing I could get my hands on. It became apparent over the years just how much of an inspiration she'd been back then. Other than that, I'm just a dumb old country boy with something to say and she's the reason I write today. I've thought of her often over the years and her impact on me was deep and profound.

Not long after quitting school, I found myself in the Karate class of Herby Black. I don't know why or how I became involved with Herby, but lucky for me I did. He not only taught Karate, but he taught the sound principles that I would struggle to make a part of my life as it moved along. His classes were never violence oriented and he stressed respect and discipline, not traits stressed in the years of Karate and Kung Fu I'd eventually take. I traveled the world and learned many things over the years, but much of what stuck with me, came from Herby Black. Really, other than my Grandfather, he was the only positive male role model I had as a boy. He was a long time officer for the Milledgeville Police Department and is now a Magistrate Judge for the State of Georgia.

I've only recently reconnected with these two people who had such an impact on my life. In retrospect, both of them were surprised by my coming forth with my admission, the ones who touch you the most always are. I think that both Ms. Bush and Mr. Black have had an influence on hundreds, if not thousands, of people over the years. They've gone through their lives ever so slightly touching so many of us and never even seen what they've done to change the world. I think that at its best, writing can change the world, but also feel I'll never make the difference people like these two have.

I've never went a day without thinking of them, but neither even remembered me when I found them. How could they, given the number of people they've dealt with over the years? Ms. Bush remembered the story, if she could have forgotten something I wish that had been it. What makes this so striking? They changed me forever and I was just one of the many they encountered. Now is the time to seek out those you'll never forget and let them in on the fact that they changed your life and the world. People should know they make a difference. This goes out to Marian C. Bush and Herbert F. Black, I hope to have even a fraction of the positive impact on the world as the two of you. Thank you for being the people you are. Not because you have to be, but simply because you are.

DON'T TRY THIS AT HOME

The Evils of Smoking

When I was 14, I had a favorite pair of pants. They were baby blue, bell bottoms, with just the right amount of fray on the cuffs and were the definition of cool. I pounced on them when they came from the dryer, wearing them as often as possible. The memory of the last time I wore them is literally burned into my mind.

My Grandpaw and I drove to the store. That was an adventure in itself. Grandpaw never broke the speed limit; in fact he never even bent it. Pulling up, we were greeted by the 10 or so old geezers that sat out front on coke crates. Now I'm one of those geezers myself and they no longer make coke crates. I feel cheated.

Once inside I went to work trying to get a dollar. Instead he wanted to buy me a coke and put it on his ticket. I needed the dollar. I worked him in the store. I continued to work him on the way back to the truck.

Finally he gave in and handed me the bill, "I know you're going to buy cigarettes. Don't let your Grandmaw see em or she'll skin us both. You better walk home."

That was fine. I'd probably beat him home anyway. I hurried inside and bought a pack, then stepped out and leaned against the building. I packed them as the old men that were gathered around stared. Why not, I was what cool is. I had on my coolest pants and my hair was longer than it had ever been. I was cooler than those old guys ever dreamed of being in their lives, they should be staring.

Oh, did I mention the pants were tight, very tight? I put a cigarette in my mouth and then reached into my pocket for one of the 20 or so strike anywhere matches I'd stolen from the top of Grandmaw's fridge. I'd been practicing and could strike them on my teeth, zipper or a fingernail, even more cool. The old men were silent, possibly anticipating entertainment.

Pulling one from my pocket, I lit my smoke. It was the coolest, single move I'd ever made. Puff one, my mind registered I hadn't lit the match. Puff two it registered that my leg was burning. Looking down, imagine my horror as black, blue and gray smoke rose from the fabric of my pants where the pocket was. Two of the matches had rubbed together inside and even though they were starved for oxygen, the sulfur was doing its job. They were going to run their course.

I screamed and flicked the offending cigarette away, then started beating at my leg. Jumping up and down, I furiously tried to stop the pain that was steadily growing. I danced as the old men started to laugh. This was the best show they'd had in years. I knew what I had to do, so dancing and hopping around on one leg I pulled the pants off and threw them to the pavement. They took this opportunity and their newfound oxygen to burst into flames. I jumped on them and stomped until they were out, in front of all those men while they roared with laughter.

I snatched them up even before they were out good and ran across the parking lot into the woods. When I finally got home, after five miles in the woods, I had a blister the size of a honeydew melon on my leg and pieces of melted polyester on my hands. I stashed the pants in the burn barrel and spent the rest of my life trying to overcome the effects that the embarrassment caused.

I'm still a smoker. I wasn't smart enough to figure that out, but if any of you doubt that smoking is evil, just consider what else would cause a 14-year-old boy to take his pants off and dance in front of a bunch of old men in public? Please keep this between us. It was embarrassing enough.

KENNESAWTAYLOR

Blind Date

Don't start laughing about me having a blind date, I really did have one. Once, in San Diego, I was temporarily stationed in a maintenance crew of about twenty guys. We didn't know each other and had only the barest of necessities.

One of the guys was from West Virginia, named Posie, that's right just like the flower. To make things worse, he was the strangest looking person I'd ever seen. He was quite round, but his arms and legs were thin as rails. He looked like a cartoon caricature and we treated him like one.

So, when the news came down that Posie's sister was going to visit and he wanted one of us to take her out for a night on the town, we all became scarce. After a few days of dread, someone decided we would draw straws. Reluctantly I participated and subsequently, lost. The day drew near as the twenty of us pulled together the required set of civilian cloths needed to pull it off. So it was that two guys forced me down the hall in borrowed clothes to meet her for our date.

She was in the lounge of our barracks surrounded by the rest of our group, who were buzzing and vying for her attention. Get this, her name was Rosie Posie. The crowd parted and standing there was this beautiful blond that resembled Marilyn Monroe. I was amazed and thought maybe I hadn't lost after all. I kissed her hand, surprising myself. She spoke softly in the smooth tones of a good southern girl. She seemed innocent, she seemed pure, things I'd missed living in California.

We caught a cab and headed for a nice little restaurant I knew was friendly to sailors. Giving me a wink she produced a bottle of Brandy from her purse.

This was getting more interesting as it went. Her demeanor changed, "Please don't say anything about this to my brother, he's so protective." I was more than glad to comply. Alarms did go off when she finished it in about five minutes.

"Hey pull over at a bottle shop will ya?" The cab driver nodded, he was only too happy to help. Running inside she came back with a new larger bottle, it took her all of ten minutes to polish it off. I was starting to have serious doubts. As we moved along she scanned her surroundings.

"Hey stop here, this is where I want to go." I didn't know the bar she was pointing at, but I knew there are places sailors don't go and this was one of them. I tried to change her mind, the cab driver pulled in, smiling at me in the mirror. She jumped out and ran inside. I reluctantly followed.

I was in enemy territory and I knew it. The only thing keeping me from getting thrown out was her looks. I knew it wouldn't last long. The bartender flirted with her, as did a steady flow of guys that took the seat on the other side of her. My being there didn't matter at all.

The last of the many guys that sat down beside her must've hit the wrong button, because suddenly she stood and proclaimed, "West by God Virginia." Then she proceeded to beat this guy like she was a man. For my part, I was no help while about ten guys beat and kicked me on the floor. When the police took me out in handcuffs for a little visit to the emergency room on the way to jail, she came out with her arm linked in another officer's arm. He was flirting with her and assuring her he would get her back to her hotel safely.

I spent a few days in jail and never told Posie what happened. She left town, telling him that I was a perfect gentleman and that she'd had a great time. Yeah, me too!

KENNESAWTAYLOR

Kick the Tires Boys

I acquired my first mini bike in 1970, I bought it used. The throttle cable was broken; it only ran at half throttle. The key switch was broken so you had to touch a wire to the plug to shut it down, which was under the seat. The problem with cables that don't work properly, and this one didn't, is that they eventually break and this one did.

Once it broke, the bike was stuck at full throttle. It'd been parked about a month waiting on a cable my Dad would never buy. One day my parents left me at 10:00 to run our gas station. Don't act like you don't believe me. Remember this was when parents believed that all children were born with more than two brain cells and expected them to act like it. This proves, I guess, they were wrong.

Anyway, three older teenagers showed up and wanted to ride. We did it sometimes when my parents were gone. We'd ride out of the parking lot, turn right and go to the other driveway, turning back into the lot and finishing at the gas pumps where we started.

"We can't, the throttle is stuck wide open." I explained.

"Watch this." said one of the biggest. He put one hand on the handlebar and reaching around behind himself, picked the back tire up. Another of them pulled the cord and it started up, the back tire spinning wildly. He plopped down and it moved across the parking lot. At the road he turned right, moved to the other driveway and turned back into the parking lot. Once he reached the pumps he stood and lifted the rear tire from the ground. Easy, I could do that, right? I watched as the other two had a successful ride.

It was my turn. I climbed on and lifted as hard as possible to convince them I could do it. They weren't impressed, but said they'd stop me when I passed by. My mind was screaming at me so loudly I couldn't think. I held the tire up, kind of, and someone yanked the cord. Across the parking lot I shot, like a bullet. What I or they had for that matter, forgotten to take into consideration, was I weighed less than they did.

By the time I hit the road I was moving too fast to make the turn. It soared to a speed it had never attained before. The wide-open road being my only option, I took it. The bike was moving above the speed it was designed for, so if I took one hand from the handlebars, it went to wobbling. My only hope was to shut her down. Reaching under the seat I fought to touch the wire to the plug, but only succeeded in electrocuting myself. It would cut out slightly and then fire back up, barely slowing.

Soon there was a truck behind me with the teenagers in it as I sped toward town about three miles away. They yelled instructions; this wasn't helping my already scared and overwhelmed mind. I could come up with no solution. My only hope now was that it would run out of gas before I made it to town. I don't know if you've figured it out yet, but my luck ain't too good.

The city had been replacing water lines all my life and on this day half of Main Street was dug up. Moving at about 47 miles an hour, I may have been able to dodge the cars and people, but the large holes and mounds of dirt were too much. Somehow I missed the first two, but the third got me. I jumped the hole and smacked head first into the dirt on the other side. The bike stuck in the bank, I fell into the hole.

I limped for a few days and as I expected, my Dad never bought that cable, which was a good thing because the bike was broken in half. I had to put bricks under it in the middle so it would sit in the garage and look normal enough for him not to notice.

Just like buying a car, if you buy a used mini bike you better kick the tires.

KENNESAW TAYLOR

It Was the Bird

This is about the last time I went camping as a boy. Before you get a picture in your mind, I feel I must explain. My best friend was Danny Defoe. He'd grown up in Atlanta and moved out into the suburbs when he was 10. He missed the city and when we were 15 he talked me into going camping with him. We arranged it so our parents thought each was spending the night with the other. Then we'd buy a bottle of brandy and drive into the city 35 miles away.

After parking the car where it would be safe, we'd disappear down the streets where the homeless lived. Secretly I was fearful, but said nothing. We'd wander the streets of Atlanta dressed in shabby clothing. We talked to the homeless and the hopelessly insane. He was always looking for a person he felt we could learn something from. He went on to be an advocate for those people after college.

Once he found someone who interested him, we'd bundle up with them in an alley or where they lived, produce the bottle and share it as we talked the rest of the night away. We had some close calls and were harassed by the police a few times, but mostly we just sat around and froze, while we listened to stories and shared the brandy. Looking back now, those were some of the best nights of my life. They kept me from ever turning away from the needy.

I remember the last time we did it. It was an especially cold night in February, I was 17. We'd gotten pretty good at finding people who had a good story to tell and who could use the brandy. On this night we found Simpson, he had a lean scruffy face that indicated that he actually shaved once in a while.

He was thin and wore several sets of clothes. His outer most garment was a flight jacket from the Korean war. We learned it wasn't really his. He had a unique way of folding newspapers to make a hat, wearing six one on top of the other, then finished it off with a blue knit toboggan with Cubs embroidered on it.

"So why are you here Simpson, man?" Danny asked as he passed the brandy his way.

Simpson said nothing, but took the bottle. A small spark danced around in his eyes, possibly the start of a tear. He turned the bottle up and sipped gingerly with his toothless mouth. Carefully he drank only a little; afraid he wouldn't get another turn if he was too greedy. I took a small sip. Danny passed it directly back to Simpson.

"Come on man, what gives?" Danny tried again.

Simpson sipped again then stuck the bottle back in my direction. I felt awful for him, he was too far-gone to even have an intelligent conversation. I declined the bottle, figuring he needed it more than I did. Slowly he turned away from us towards the drum behind him, with a fire in it. I looked towards Danny and shrugged my shoulders, he just shook his head. I started to get up, we'd struck out with Simpson.

We almost missed his first words they were so soft.

"I killed her," he said. We settled back down as he turned the bottle up again. We glanced at each other, "we had a bird you see."

"No we don't see, tell us about it." Danny said, trying to spur him on.

"She was a beautiful bird and I know you think old Simpson is crazy, but she talked." He turned up the bottle and pulled hard from it.

"Not like you think. She talked to me, she helped me with things. I thought I was losing my mind and then, I though she might be God. I was in love with her." His body slumped and after a time he pulled up the bottle and finished it off.

"One day when I got home from work she described in great detail how my wife had an affair while I was gone." Turning, he rummaged around in a pile of old clothing and newspapers until he produced a large bottle of wine. Turning back to us he offered it half heartily. We declined; he turned back to the drum and drank deeply.

"I could hardly believe it and denied it for months, but the damn bird kept at me. I killed her."

"You killed the bird?" Danny asked, but in my stomach I knew it was the wrong question. Simpson sat, his shaking shoulders only steadying when he took a pull from the bottle of wine.

"No, I loved that bird. I lost everything, including the bird. It was the damn bird's fault."

We looked at each other and stood slowly. We'd heard many stories over the years, but were pretty sure this was one we could've missed. We moved from the alley leaving him there.

"He's just crazy." I said

"No, he was telling the truth."

"So what do we do?"

"We gotta tell the cops."

Within two blocks we spotted a cop and told him what we'd heard. "Stay here and I'll get back to you in a minute." he said.

We stood there and watched as a wagon arrived and placed Simpson inside, then disappeared before he could find us again.

The Atlanta Journal ran this headline the next morning: Local Police Arrest Murderer. The story explained that Jonas Simpson had killed his wife five years earlier. He had dismembered her into small pieces that would fit into gallon sized bags and put her in the freezer. He then disappeared and she wasn't found until the power was turned off and the smell alerted the neighbors.

That was our last camping trip. We had no heart for it after that. Today I defend people like Jonas.

KENNESAW TAYLOR

The Ride

When I was 14, my stepfather was killed in front of me. If you've read my book, you know it was the first day I had hopes of living to adulthood. During that year several other key things happened. I had to quit school and go to work full time. I also inherited a 750 Triumph motorcycle, until my Mother was forced to sell it. She replaced it with a smaller one. It was a good thing in the end because if I dropped it, in no world could I ever pick it back up. I drove to work or wherever I wanted to go at 14, it was a different world back then.

I worked at a textile mill and worked 12 hour shifts. So I was off three days a week. The burden of life was settling in pretty hard, so I took to riding on long journeys when I was off. It didn't cost much and it gave me time to figure out what was going on. I would just pick a direction and drive for a day and a half, then turn around and drive back, sleeping in a park somewhere when I needed to. The scenery and towns passed along while I was lost in the thoughts of a grown 14 year old.

Even with all I'd seen in my life, I was to learn a few more lessons. This was the trip I would learn them and it would be my last. I found myself in Mississippi. I always traveled the back roads. I eased off the road to get a drink. The store was old and the gas pumps had glass balls on top. The parking lot was dirt and the store looked like it was standing only out of habit. Old trucks and cars were parked haphazardly around the lot.

My hair was halfway down my back and I'd been on the road for a couple days, so I looked pretty bad. Coming in from the sun the store was dark and it was a shotgun shack, narrow and deep. I walked to the cooler and got one of those cokes in the little green bottles. I didn't notice all the locals sitting in the back of the store on coke crates, but they noticed me. As I was paying, the storeowner said nothing to me. However the yahoo's in the back were whistling, and making comments about how pretty a girl I was. I knew that this innocent stop had gone horribly wrong and chugged the coke as I made my way to the door.

When I exited the building, I dropped what was left in the trashcan and headed for the bike. I could hear the crates falling over and shuffling of feet and cursing going on behind me. I only weighed 120 pounds so it took every bit of it to get the bike fired up. Usually it was hard and took several tries, not that day. I had a reason to get it right the first time. I hit the pavement spinning tires and almost lay her down right there. I didn't have my helmet or glasses on. I could see the trucks and cars coming from the parking lot in a cloud of dust behind me in the mirror.

I pushed her to about 80, the fastest I'd ever been, thinking they would give up, but instead they gained on me. I took a right onto a dirt road and almost lost her again. I was only out of sight for a moment, so I turned, jumped the ditch and once I was out in the woods deep enough, I lay her down. Pulling leaves over the bike I tried to hide the chrome so they wouldn't see me and I lay back to watch the road.

The rest of the day I lay in the woods and watched as 2 trucks and a car, all of which looked like they weren't legal to be on the road, drove up and down the dirt road looking for me. They got more drunk as the day moved on. Into the night they drove, calling out to this pretty little girl in the woods, shining spotlights. Sometime in the middle of the night they gave up and went away.

I pushed dirt under the bike, then lifted it a little and kicked more under it. It took me several hours to get it to a standing position, but by daylight I had it and fired her up. I never stopped and moved at a quicker pace than ever. I was never more glad to see the state of Georgia.

The moral of this story or something is: I was 15, it had been less than a year since I'd watched my stepfather die. I'd had to quit school and go to work full time. I was so patriotic that I reeked of it and would go on to join the service at the earliest possible moment. I was being harassed and hunted like a dog in my own Country. If they had caught me, I would probably never have been seen again. I fully learned the word prejudice lying there in those Mississippi leaves that night and I never forgot it. Those who hate, hate for no real reason, they make it up as they go. Sometimes I think we've come a long way, sometimes I think we've not moved at all.

The Meanest Shotgun I Ever Met

I only visited my uncle in the Georgia Mountains about three times while I was growing up. Go figure, every time I did, he wanted to visit his brother-in-law who lived only thirty miles from my house. His family lived in the woods in a house that had never known the luxury of a coat of paint. It had a porch that ran all the way around it. The washing machine was one of those old, manual, roller types and sat on the back porch. Right beside it was the bathtub. If that wasn't enough, you had to watch your step because the porch had weak spots. The toilet was an outhouse. The house was set up like a lot of old houses with all the rooms tied together. No halls, just two doors in every room. The only heat was a wood stove and the blankets on the bed were so thick that they held you down once you climbed in and you woke up just the way you went to sleep.

They had a son named Vincent, who was about sixteen. He had long, straight black hair, which made him cool to me. I was only fourteen at the time. Later in life I realized he had long, straight, black, dirty hair. Taking a bath on the back porch in the winter time tends to make you take baths less often than others might.

One day everybody went to town except Vincent and me. If I haven't mentioned it yet, he could get me into trouble in a flat minute.

"Look, my Paw's got this shotgun in the closet, names Old Bill. It belonged to my grandfather. Wanna shoot it?"

"I don't know."

"Oh, you can't handle a shotgun yet."

"I can too."

"It's a sixteen-gauge."

"No it's not. I've shot lots of shotguns and I've never heard of a sixteen-gauge."

"See, I knew you didn't know anything about guns."

"I do, get it out. I wanna see it."

So we dug around in the room until we could get to the closet door and get it out. It was the oldest gun I'd seen and it said sixteen- gauge right on the barrel. All the while he was steady conning me into shooting it. I had shot twelve-gauge guns before and I knew that they kicked pretty hard. It made sense that this would kick harder.

"I better not."

"I'll show you a way."

We went into the barn, which had a gate at one end that opened into the pasture. The gate was made of two by sixes.

"Just put your shoulder on this side of a board and put the gun on the other side, that way the board will protect you."

This was at least a way I could keep from looking like a chicken. We loaded old Bill and I put my left shoulder against the gate, put the gun on the other side, took aim at nothing in particular and pulled the trigger. The gun erupted, throwing me on my back in the hay. Two other things happened. It broke the gate down and set the hay inside the barn on fire. I thought it had broken my arm. Vincent was yelling and trying to contain the fire before it burned down the barn. The horses didn't care much for the fire and could see freedom as the gate was gone. Somehow we got everything under control.

"Holy cow! I've never tried to shoot that thing. My dad won't even shoot it anymore and I didn't think you'd really do it."

There are things you should and things you shouldn't do. Learning to tell the difference between the two is the hard part. Old Bill was a good teacher and the meanest shotgun I ever met.

KENNESAW TAYLOR

FOOD AND DRINK

The Drink!

I never figured out why they call the water on Navy bases the drink, but they do. The drink is a place you never want to be, even in the best of ports the drink is filthy. In some ports if you fall in and you're seen, you must get a shot for every disease known to man, all at one time. I have had my share of drink experiences. While in Napier, New Zealand the water was so pure that some of us started jumping off the mast into the drink. You could see the bottom and it was probably at least 50 feet deep, we couldn't help ourselves. The officer of the day had a fit when he realized we were jumping out over the side of the ship from about 70 feet up. He should have written us all up but didn't and we realized that the Navy didn't care for such activities. The next time I found myself in the drink was not nearly as much fun but a whole lot funnier.

It was getting near to the end of my time in the Navy, so I had become a little bit crazier than I was when I first enlisted. The night started with me being broke, which meant that we still had a week until payday. We got paid every two weeks and everyone was broke the second week. I had planned on staying onboard and preparing for an inspection the next morning. I wasn't ready at all and needed the time anyway. It was then that Jim asked if I wanted to have some beers, I declined saying that I was broke. Jim insisted and said he had some money and he was buying. I told him that I had a lot to do and really should stay onboard. He said that he didn't have much money anyway, so we wouldn't be late and he really didn't want to drink alone. Hey, I had to say yes, it was my duty, so we got dressed and hit San Diego.

Well I realized soon that he had more money than he let on, because the beer just kept on coming. Soon the bar was closed and we were walking down the street with our arms around each other singing (Girl you really got me going) by Van Halen. We were just like drunken sailors in the movies; we could barely walk.

After walking all the way to the base, Jim decided that he had enough money to get a cab from the gate to the ship, maybe a mile. So we climbed into one of the many cabs that hung around the gate for that purpose and off we went, drunk as fools. About half way across the base, Jim admitted to me that he was broke and I about died right there in the back seat. "What will we do?" I asked. Just do what I do he said. We were on pier 8 and at pier 7 he told the driver that this was the place. As soon as the driver stopped, he threw the door open, made about 3 happy little bounces with a smile on his face and jumped 30 feet into the drink. It was three o'clock in the morning, we were drunk as hell and I was dumbfounded. The driver, who was from the Middle East somewhere, was as shocked as I was. He didn't move for a minute, then he started cussing the Navy and America in broken English, then he started reaching for me over the seat. I had to decide right now, so I escaped his grasp, slid out of the car and in 3 steps I was jumping into the darkness myself.

Jim had waited for me and we laughed hard as we started towards pier 8. If I remember correctly it was about 200 yards to where we were headed. So we took our time and laughed and joked while we floated, we could still hear the guy yelling at us about it only being a $1.50. We swam the whole way and were still drunk as we climbed onto pier 8 soaking wet and laughing at the driver, whom we couldn't hear anymore. We were surprised to see shore patrol waiting for us and given the gravity of the situation we still couldn't control our laughter. I mean, there we were, drunk as hell, wet as hell and the shore patrol guys were laughing their butts off. The whole while the driver was cussing at such a speed that only about every 10th word was English. When we finally got ourselves under control, the shore patrol guys complemented us on our slick escape and asked the driver what would make him happy. Realizing that he was out numbered he said he just wanted his money. We didn't have it all, so the shore patrol guys, just happy that we had given them a laugh on an otherwise boring watch, decided to help.

The only problem was, between the four of us; we couldn't come up with the $1.50 we owed. So they decided that we would go on the ship, bum the money from someone on the quarterdeck and pay the driver. When the five of us got on the ship, Jim and I realized that we knew everybody on watch. One of them demanded to know, in a serious voice, what this was all about, so we proceeded to tell them in the most comical way possible. By the time we got to the jumping in the drink part, everyone was laughing so hard that we had tears in our eyes. So now you've got the 3 guys on watch, the shore patrol guys and us two laughing to the point of rolling on the deck. The driver was not a happy camper and refused the money. He demanded to see the Captain and had that right.

So at about 4 o'clock, when nothing else could be worked out, the officer of the watch went to wake up the Captain, we were all still laughing. The Captain showed up in khakis and a T-shirt, mad as a hornet. He talked to the cabby, who now rarely said one word of English, then turned to us with a confused look on his face. "What the hell is going on here Kay?" No one had laughed at all since his arrival, so then I retold the story, embellishing it all the more, but at attention the whole time. The whole time I was telling the story, everyone in the bunch, except the driver was crying trying to hold back the laughter. The Captain had his back to the driver, tears were rolling down his face and his lips were quivering, but he never made a sound. As a true gentleman and a good officer, he turned to the driver and said in a calm voice, "What must we do to make you happy?" The driver said he just wanted his money, so he pulled out $1.50 and paid the driver.

He then chewed us out for about 30 minutes and told us to get ready for the inspection. I went to the inspection at 7 o'clock in my cleanest, dirty pair of dungarees, straight out of the dirty clothes, wrinkles and all. No shave, no bath and smelling like a brewery. I could barely stand up, but I passed and we never heard anything about that night again. We never even paid back the money but everyone on the ship knew about it the next day. We laughed about it every time we got drunk for a while and I doubt I will ever forget it. I can still hear the driver yelling out over the water, "Hey! American! It's only a $1.50!

Public Restroom

Recently I admitted to all of you that I set my pants on fire and danced in my drawers in front of a bunch of old men. I'm still wondering why I told you that. While not funny at the time, it seems to be now. At 14 I thought it was the most embarrassing thing that could happen to a person; at 20 I found out I was wrong.

I arrived at a party in Jacksonville Fl., having already made financial contributions to at least three, different beer companies and at least two, Kentucky distilleries. I probably thought myself suave and debonair, more likely I had a stupid grin on my face. I mean really, stupid people shouldn't drink.

I mingled, but my real mission was to have a drink in both hands at the same time. Quickly, I accomplished my immediate goal in life. I'm going back right now and underline, stupid people shouldn't drink. Soon, as it always happens, I knew I'd need to find the bathroom. I found it on the back wall of the room the party was in. It stood there open. By that I mean, one of the fifty people in the room had ripped the door off and it stood leaning against the wall near by. My befuddled mind, my two drinks and my over full bladder as a group, struggled to come up with a sane solution.

The house was old, so the door was thick and made of solid wood. It appeared to be heavy. I watched for a while as a few other men went inside, pulled the door over the opening, carefully leaning it at the right angle so it would stay there and come back out with no problem. Still I hesitated, dancing near the wall alone with two drinks in my hands. My bladder doubted my intelligence. My drinks were getting hot and my mind was calling me names I didn't deserve. In fact, I still hold a grudge about it today. Just who does he think he is anyway?

Finally, a few girls took their turns. If they could do it, surely I could, too. Stumbling along, I tried to play down the fact of where I was headed. Sitting my drinks down I positioned the door against the opening, prepared myself, picked up my two drinks and decided to leave aiming to chance. I turned up one of my drinks. It occurred to me that you really only rent beer. It also occurred to me that I really didn't appreciate the part of the beer industry I represented.

About the time I was fully engrossed in the natural function I'd put off for far, too long, there was a tremendous explosion. Well, I wish it had been an explosion. What it turned out to be was that big, heavy door falling flat out onto the real wood floor of the old house. It sounded like a cannon went off. Out of fear someone knocked the needle off of whatever was playing on the record player at the time (yes, I said record player), with a ziiiiiiip and the party fell completely silent.

As if those two things weren't enough to happen at the same time, two other things also happened. For my part, I jerked around to see what was after me. So there I stood with a beer in one hand and another in guzzle mode. Already started, my natural function was going to run its course, beer going in one end, puddle on the floor coming out the other while I stared into the faces of fifty people. The door falling in such a dramatic fashion had, of course, made everyone in the room look to see what had happened. To make matters worse, no one turned away, but stared on instead.

Ok God, message sent, message received. I didn't withdraw my financial support from the beer companies that night, but it wasn't long after that. Again, stupid people shouldn't drink; I was just barely smart enough to stop when I did.

KENNESAW TAYLOR

Assault and Battery

I was in Seattle in 1978, still wet behind the ears and hadn't even started to drink yet. Seattle was to be the jumping off point for an around the world cruise on a destroyer. I was pretty excited about it.

We had about a month to goof off because the ship was undergoing repairs. We worked all day, but at night were free to go out. One night four of us went to the small China town in downtown to a theatre to watch kung fu movies. It was an all night slugfest. We sat there from about 4pm until 3am and watched one movie after the other. It was all in Chinese and we couldn't understand a word, but hey, who cared? Well, at some point even Bruce Lee has to eat, so we stepped out and headed for a store. A sack full of burritos and a 12 pack of beer seemed like a good idea, so that's what we had.

We stood in the alley in a bad part of town and gobbled down the burritos and drank the beer. Only one of us was old enough or experienced enough to be drinking in the first place. Our young eyes watched our surroundings carefully while we ate and drank hurriedly. No one said it, but each of us secretly hoped we'd be attacked. We'd just watched so much violence, we thought we were supermen. After a few beers and burritos we were probably as close to it as we'd ever been. With the buzz only a novice drinker can get out of two or three beers, we decided to walk the ten miles back to the boat instead of getting a cab.

We moved through the roughest part of the city at 4am, openly dragging for someone to decide to mug us. We talked excitedly while we moved along and indeed we were strung pretty tight. I believed then and I believe now, we could've given a street gang a run for their money. We'd just been through boot camp and I'd been taking karate for a couple of years before joining. The city moved on as we passed through it and soon we were on the waterfront, which was pretty much deserted at that time of night. We felt cheated as we moved along. Fighting each other was about all we had left and we weren't going to do that. We'd just walked right through the roughest part of town, the part you were never to walk through at night, unmolested.

Our buzz was just starting to wear off a little when the guy in front, Judd was his name, he was short, redheaded and from New York City. He was the oldest and meanest of the four of us. He jumped up and placed a perfect roundhouse kick right to the head of a telephone pole. I have no idea what the pole did to provoke him, but he sure picked the wrong one to mess with. Instantly the four of us attacked the pole. We put up a good fight for what must have been 15 minutes, kicking and punching this poor pole, trying to beat it into submission. At some point we heard something and looked across the road. There was the coast guard base and at the gate sat a little glass shack with two Coast Guard guys in it. They were laughing so hard they were rolling around on the road outside of the building.

Felling pretty stupid we moved off toward the ship assessing our wounds. We had tar all over our clothes, cuts and bruises all over our legs and fists and somehow one of us had gotten the start of a pretty good, black eye from our encounter. The pole had been tougher than we thought. We nearly made it to the ship before the Seattle police picked us up. I guess we weren't too hard to spot; the pole had beaten us up pretty badly. We weren't drunk, but the officer had no sense of humor, so standing on the quarterdeck of our ship he arrested us for assault and battery.

It seemed none of the police had a sense of humor because they pushed it for two weeks before a judge threw it out, releasing us to leave on the ship when it pulled out. All charges were dropped, but we left the courtroom with a stern warning to never assault a telephone pole in Seattle again. I never have, I can't speak for the others.

KENNESAWTAYLOR

Mamma Lied

First let me say that I never understood a time when I didn't appreciate girls. I see it in the movies and on TV, but I have a hard time believing that little boys really pass through a stage where they don't like girls, if they do I certainly didn't. I'm sorry if this sounds bad, but women make the world go round and I like it that way.

In the summer of 1966, when I was 6 years old, we lived in Bentley Subdivision in Milledgeville. I was in love with the girl next door. I think it turned out to be about a two year thing. That is a shout out to Margaret, because I've never forgotten her and never will. I've always done the cooking and I guess it must have started that summer, however disastrous it turned out.

I decided to cook some hot dogs for the girls of the neighborhood. So after liberating some hot dogs from captivity and stealing a few matches, I rounded up a few girls and headed out into the woods behind our house. Even then I was trying to use cooking for evil, it set a bad precedent. We moved up into the woods and found a little spot that wasn't visible to any houses. This was the first time I ever started a fire. I pushed a bunch of dried leaves into a pile in the middle of woods that were thick with them and struck a match.

I remember very distinctly that I didn't know how to start a fire. I remember being scared that I wouldn't be able to do it now that I had an audience. That's another one of God's lessons or little cruelties perhaps. If you need to start a fire to keep from freezing it can be very hard. If you don't want to start one, well it'll just jump up and burn at the first chance it gets. I only had to consider for a moment that I might not get it started, because I swear before the match even hit the leaves it took off.

This was my first fire, my first attempt at cooking, but it was also my first chance to try out my dancing skills. I danced and stomped at the fire. The girls took off headed to get help instead of helping. I don't think it would've mattered I'd never have put it out anyway. It was going to town in a fast car and I wasn't driving. I stayed with it as long as I had the nerve and then took off for the house.

I slipped through the woods, avoiding my mother and other women of the neighborhood as they made their way to the fire, now burning out of control. I went straight to my mother's room, the only one with a lock on the door and locked myself in. There was no fire department to call back then, all the men were gone to work. So as I cowered in her room, she and the other women fought that fire in the heat of the summer trying to save the whole area.

She and two others were pregnant. Lord it's a wonder that no babies were lost that day. It took them over two hours to get it under control and put out. I'd sat in her room shaking the whole time. My little sister kept coming down and sitting outside the door giving me progress reports. I had it in my mind that the door would never open again and I was content to just stay in that room for the rest of my life.

Soon after it was out my mother was at the door demanding that I open it. No way, I knew better. She changed tactics and started trying to sweet talk me, still I wouldn't give in. She then changed again and convinced my sister that she knew it was an accident and that she wasn't going to beat me. Moving away from the door she left my four-year-old sister to get me out of my hiding place. My sister believed she wasn't going to beat me and soon made a believer out of me. I opened the door and walked into the living room sheepishly.

She stood there covered in soot, face blackened and sweaty. She smelled strongly of smoke. She also beat the mess out of me. I'll never forget how clammy she felt as she swung blindly making any contact she could. The smell of smoke was being firmly embedded in my memory at that moment in my life.

I learned several lessons that day. God doesn't care just how cold you are, you'll work for a fire if you need one. God will teach you some big lessons with a match, a few leaves and some stolen hot dogs. Oh yeah the biggest one, Mamma's will tell a lie in a minute when they need to.

The Ivey General Coffee Club

There's nothing new about the more seasoned of us getting together at some local gathering place every morning and passing the time by telling tall tales. When I was a young boy in Baldwin County, it was a store on Sparta Highway called Aides Groceries. Every day you could count on there being about ten or so old men sitting around out front on Coke crates, telling things that would make your ears curl if you believed about half of it.

The older I get, the more I find myself having coffee with that crowd. It not only happens at Ivey General Store, it happens at the Texaco in Gordon and it used to happen at the Chicken House and will no doubt happen there again when the reconstruction is completed. In the evening, it happens at the Huddle House right out in front for all the world to see. Now, when I was younger, I thought they were just a bunch of old geezers, with nothing else to do. Now that I'm approaching the old geezer status, I've found that to be exactly what we are.

Most pass them by and try not to get dragged into whatever tall tale or gossip that happens to be the main topic of conversation for that morning's session. Over the years I've walked around them on many occasions, just to avoid being sucked in or asked to participate. If they ever ask you a question, it was only designed to bolster one opinion over the other and add fuel to the argument already going before you arrived. In fact, most of the time your answer would be wrong no matter what you said.

Then one year I was having a hard time with my tomato plants. So after ordering a sausage biscuit, I gingerly approached the two tables in the front of Ivey General and was amazed that they made room for me to have a seat. After all, I'm only about fifty, still a child. A couple of the regulars argued back and forth about the impending election, that was the main topic for a while. Everyone present doubted the integrity, patriotism and lineage of both candidates. I believe they may have even insulted both of their mothers a few times.

I chewed at my breakfast, trying to get up the nerve to jump into the conversation, but I sure didn't want to be in the one they were currently having.

"Hey, I put out about ten tomato plants this year and they don't seem to be doing well." I said. The tables fell silent for a moment. I went back to eating my breakfast, wishing I hadn't said anything at all.

Shortly one of them started and told me all about the soil in this area and what I needed to do. Then another called him an old fool and told me how he would do it. I sat there for an hour as they bantered back and forth, covering everything known to man about tomatoes.

That's when I realized that sitting at those two tables were hundreds of years of combined knowledge and life experience about any subject you could come up with. I find myself now when I have the time, eating breakfast with them fairly often. Sometimes you need to be wearing hip waders to save your shoes, but most times you learn something that will serve some purpose in the future. They argue and call each other names, not to be repeated here, but behind all that, they're friends that have endured a long shared struggle with the land, the chalk mines and the good and bad deeds of other family members over the years.

So the next time you have a question about anything life throws at you, find one of these coffee clubs and have a seat. You may learn some things you never wanted to know, but you may just learn the answer to all of life's questions.

KENNESAW TAYLOR

Meatloaf

You could not force me to eat meatloaf when I was a child and I mean, I grew up hard, but meatloaf never crossed my lips. The threat of a beating would make me do many things. An actual beating would pretty much cover everything else. I mean things like unstopping toilets, touching dirty diapers, moving things that could be filled with spiders, moving the dead snake out of the yard and even killing a litter of puppies that came down with rabies with a shotgun once. Oh yeah and who could forget kissing Aunt Ruby.

Just a raised hand would usually cover the normal stuff. Chitterlings, greens of any kind, the fat from a steak, broccoli, cauliflower, cooked carrots and who can forget my personal favorite, green beans. Yuck!

I was beaten into unconsciousness once for refusing to eat meatloaf. Guess what? You can't eat meatloaf if you're not awake. It was just too easy to hide things in meatloaf, things like onions, bell peppers and just anything you're trying to sneak on an unsuspecting child.

After many years overseas I became accustomed to eating almost anything. I've eaten things that even I shudder at the memories of. Worse yet I'm sure, I've eaten things that to this day I'll never know what they were. The secret to losing your eating inhibitions I found was for some pretty little girl to smile sweetly and offer it to you. It worked all over the world. Well, a case of beer didn't hurt either.

When I came back from my travels there were still two things I wouldn't do. I'm afraid that says bad things about me. I would not eat meatloaf or drink after anyone. Now I'm getting older and there are more things I won't do. Wait a minute; what I mean is I've just gotten too old to do them. That still says bad things about me. I resisted meatloaf through my first wife. It wasn't that hard, our marriage was annulled in like 28 days. It turned out that the Navy found out she was still married to her first two husbands. I was easily fooled, she just wanted the benefits from marrying a sailor, but she didn't make me eat meatloaf. I was able to keep up my meatloaf beliefs for a couple more years and then it happened.

I married the woman of my dreams. She actually did the cooking for the first six months, one day I came home to find meatloaf sitting on the table. As it happened years earlier when that sweet little girl with those sweet little fingers pointed meatloaf at me, I opened my mouth and took the bite she offered. As I remember I even licked the juice from her fingers. Love makes you stupid doesn't it? Meatloaf is proof positive.

Wait, something's wrong, this is good. She uses mozzarella cheese in her meatloaf and it's the recipe I've used from that day forth. Suddenly I couldn't get enough meatloaf and we had it every week for years. What I didn't expect and what I still can't explain is that from then until now, every time I go into a restaurant and meatloaf is on the menu I order it. It's the same way with spaghetti.

I've eaten both all over the Country and I've got to tell you its bad 99% of the time, still I keep ordering it. It's like a train or car wreck. When you pass by you try not to look, so does everyone else that's holding up traffic and causing additional wrecks at the scene, but you just can't stop yourself. A meatloaf sandwich with a little mayo, man that's heaven. I can't believe I said that, I must have lost my mind.

What I have found to be true is that if you eat meatloaf at regular people's houses, it's really good. I think the problem is that, unlike what most people believe, meatloaf actually is expensive to make and restaurants can't afford to make it on a large scale and make it good. I'm not saying I never find good meatloaf at a restaurant; it's just rare when you do. And about the time you get to liking it, they change the recipe and you've got to give it up again.

With all that said, just a little advice, when it comes to meatloaf just say no. If you ever pick up the habit it's hard to break.

SHORT STORIES

The Woman Who Carries Water

Sam moved along the well worn path. He was finding it more important to rely on trees to keep him in an upright position. He'd fallen a couple times in the last year, it seemed his old legs, now 97 summers old hadn't realized that his body wasn't that old yet. He steadied himself on the tree, his tree, a huge oak that had been huge even when he was a child. Back then the exposed roots on the side facing the river had been a good place to fish and sit, one being just big enough to make a good seat. This had been where he'd spent many hours of his life, when he'd had time. The tree he'd named Galilahi, beautiful. The exposed roots of Galilahi had grown too, into a chair that sat perfectly as if the Great Spirit had grown this chair just for Sam.

There was a girl chosen every year to carry water up the bank to the village. It was her job to move water from the river to the village, not over 50 feet away in a clay pot that sat on her head. Many summers ago when Sam was still a young brave, one had fallen in and not being able to swim had drowned. Then there had come into being a water boy, to watch the water girl lest she share the same fate.

Once Sam got too old to hunt and since he was at the river all of his free time, he soon became the man who watched the woman who carries the water and had held that job now for 22 summers. While on the land he was clumsy and apt to hurt himself, when he slipped into the fast moving water to cool off he was still like a fish and swam across and back many times each day. Sam had been through many women who carried water. He had watched the years slip away as they carried pot after pot. He had watched the years slip away as they had become women, he felt as if they were all his children and they thought of him with the same kind of love.

This year the girl chosen was Amadahy, Forest Water, her mother had brought her into this world to be the woman who carries water, indeed had been one herself and one of Sam's favorites. She was old for the job, almost 20 summers, the Chief had resisted the demands of her mother for much too long just to show her he was the Chief and to be the water carrying woman you had to be untouched by any man. The Braves of the tribe who wanted her hand, had sided with the mother and the Chief was swayed.

Amadahy appeared early for her first trip, clay pot on head. No smile, all about what she was to do for an entire year. She moved along the path that would be too steep if it went straight to the water, so it was worn diagonally across the bank to make it maneuverable. It ended near where Sam sat. When she reached Sam she gave him a smile, albeit a slight one. She moved out across the 3 feet of exposed roots and gingerly filled the pot. Carefully pulling the pot back across the roots she teetered slightly, almost losing her balance. Regaining her balance she attained the path and standing up, she placed the clay pot on her head. She gave Sam a triumphant smile, turned and moved up the path.

Each step a little water sloshed out of the pot, each trip her dress became more soaked, the water making it more translucent as the day progressed.

Sam had watched this as a young man with the lust of a young man's eyes. Now it was just a thing of beauty, a thing to thank the Great Spirit for.

Amadahy for her part was the most beautiful water-carrying woman he had ever watched. When she climbed out onto the roots her hair hung long in front of her face, it was full and thicker than most and it was hard not to notice it's shine in the sunlight. Her dress slipped up to allow just a hint of her thigh, Sam decided within a few trips, the best he'd ever seen. When she stood tall and lifted the jar above her head, her grace and fitness was extraordinary, her dress clung to her body seductively. Moving back up the path her leg and calve muscles rippled from the weight of her load, further enhancing her beauty.

Her color was that of the finest Cherokee woman he'd ever seen. It was lovely in the morning light and its allure did not dim as the light did when the day came to a close. Her facial features were so soft they made his heart hurt for the man he used to be, made him think about his own woman, who had been called away by the Great Sprit many summers ago. Her beauty had been legendary among the Cherokee for many years, but even she would never compare to this woman he watched now.

As the days moved along and she became accustomed to the job she would suffer through the heat and cold of a whole year with, her smiles became bigger and soon she had a kind word for Sam at every dip of the pot. There had been few over the years that hated their job and complained at every dip or simply said nothing to this old fool sitting in the tree roots. He and Amadahy became friends, became almost lovers with their bantering back and forth so many times a day, not physical lovers, but lovers that would never be. Lovers, only through words of his youth long ago forgotten and inspired this one last time by this rare beauty of a girl. Within the year they became family and Sam found himself asking in the morning and then thanking the Great Sprit in the evening for the one more day he got to watch the woman who carries the water.

As the year progressed Sam knew this would be the last woman who carries the water he would ever watch. Amadahy knew it too and began meeting him at his hut to help him to the water's edge, to sit under his lovely tree. She knew he was past the point of helping her if she fell into the swift river, but said nothing to anyone. As the day came to a close she struggled to get him back up the bank to his bed. She never complained, she became the first and only woman who carries water, who carried the boy, who watches the woman who carries water.

Sam watched her beauty pass him many times every day for the whole year and never tired of it or the soul it was attached to. He knew she would become someone that would live forever more in the history of the Cherokee. Her name would be spoken until time ran away into a future that he would never know.

The year was long, the job was hard, but the last duty was for Amadahy to pass the clay pot to the new woman who carries water, she was 12 at most. After helping Sam to his roots just a little early she completed her job with a small ceremony.

The young girl moved down the path with much uncertainty, she navigated the roots and had her own little moment of fear, but it passed. Her thigh too was exposed a little too much for her own comfort. Standing tall she lifted the pot above her head and looked to Sam for approval, but there was none to be had. The Great sprit had turned Sam into a butterfly and he slowly lifted on the warm summer air currents and drifted off into another world. The man who became the boy who watches the woman who carries the water was no more.

KENNESAWTAYLOR

Wood Wraith!

I started in Maine to finish near home. I started late, it would be cold; around Christmas when I was done. What exactly was done? Would I get the Appalachian Trail or would it get me? I stacked the deck against myself. Would I stumble down Springer Mountain renewed, ready for an ordinary life? Would I freeze and die? I had no preference. I began the day of my divorce, taking one week to administrate my trip. I was Ill prepared, mentally weak, corpulent, with inadequate equipment. Still, my mind insisted, my wounded sprit was an eager volunteer.

Six months, two thousand miles and a lot of crying later, I had avoided others whenever possible. I slept alone in the woods and went into town for food only when starving. I'm now a more fit 44-year-old. I thought about life, my wife and her new dentist husband (she was more avarice than she appeared).

December 24, 1984

I awoke early. Cracking and sputtering, my fire battled the extreme cold. I sat wrapped in everything I owned as the fire thawed my boots. My coffeepot, just in arms reach, was brewing; little wisps of steam drifted up and away. Sipping my cup I looked out into the woods through steam and lightly falling snow. The beautiful landscape conflicted with my feeling of depression. Packing quickly, I stumbled to the trail and started up Springer.

My legs burned, my breath strained and my moustache was frozen. The snow was falling rapidly; the trail shimmered and disappeared. I kept falling and was thoroughly bruised. This was the last day; tonight a real bed. Nine more miles and then what? Revelation: I was looking forward to making it.

I heard a whimper and off to my left an orange spot on the snow. With a start I jumped from the trail, slipping towards the backpack. I rolled it over; finding it was attached to a person.

It was a her, a small wraith like girl. She was tall, thin and pale, with pastel hair. I stood up in shock. Aside from everything else she was glowing, setting everything around her alight. She was in living color. I hadn't noticed, but everything had been black and white for months. The world started glowing again and it was emanating from her. She looked foreign - French, Norwegian perhaps. Even in distress she was smiling, but apprehension was spreading on her face.

"I'm sorry, but you surprised me." My communication skills were a little rusty. "My name is Charlie, they call me Sailor."

"Man am I glad to see you. I think my ankle is broken. My trail name's Gazelle."

"Fitting name. So how bad is it?"

"It's bad, I've twisted it twice, this time it's broken."

"Well I tell ya what little Gazelle, you'll be OK. We'll hold up here and tomorrow we'll mosey down to civilization."

"Come on Sailor," she said, her voice low, "it's 18 degrees, snowing like hell; we're on top of Springer and nine miles from anywhere."

I took her hand and she held on tight. I saw fear in her eyes.

"I can do this; trust me. Besides, what choice do you have?"

My voice masked my doubt. Rummaging through my pack I found some painkillers.

"Take a couple of these. I'll have to move you around a little."

She didn't argue and swallowed them.

Working quickly I set up my tent and with effort dragged her inside. I lay our bags together and worked her onto them. I started to remove her outer clothing, first coat then shirt. I wanted her to be in her thermals, inside the bags. As I lifted her to remove her shirt our faces were close. It was surprisingly sensual, almost a lovers embrace. She smiled and I could see the pills had done their job.

Her voice was slurred.

"You wouldn't take advantage of a lame Gazelle would you?"

Our embrace tightened.

"Never little Gazelle, get some sleep, you're safe."

"Good."

I could feel and see her body beneath her thermals. I did notice, but she seemed an Angel to me. I could never hurt her. I lay her back on the bags and started zipping.

"Wait." she said giddily.

"Get my parcel, I gotta have it." I dug around finding a package of brown paper and string.

"That's it."

She sat back up.

"What is it?"

"It's a chemise, I was going to wear it tonight when I slept in a real bed."

I slipped it over her thermals, lay her down and zipped her up. Again she grabbed my hand.

"Don't leave me."

"I won't leave you, but I do have things to do. Saint Nicholas is watching you."

She giggled and said, "Nooooo, not Santa."

"No...Saint Nicholas was the patron saint of sailors, virgins and thieves."

"Oops."

"Don't worry I'm a sailor, that's good enough. Now go to sleep."

I was spending Christmas Eve in a tent on a mountain, trying to save a girl half my age. Sad, but this might be the best Christmas I'd ever had.

The cold was numbing, but I accomplished my tasks quickly. I climbed into the tent, undressed and wiggled in beside her. I smelled too much like me, she smelled too much like her. But when mixed, the scent coming from inside our bags was comfortable and earthy. She cuddled up close and looked into my eyes.

"I could wake up like this for a couple of weeks."

"I don't know what that means," I said.

"I don't really know myself. Let's take some time to see what it does mean."

"Shhhh, go to sleep. You're talking crazy."

She smiled again, drifting away. Two bodies, two bags and all we owned spent the night sheaved together, to live or die as God saw fit.

Christmas during our slow decent, I didn't bring up what was said. Hell she was drugged, why would she want me? At Amicalola State Park, rangers called a helicopter to fly her out. Strapped to the gurney she grabbed my hand.

"I meant every word; I owe you my life."

"A bad reason to get involved with somebody, don't you think?"

"Maybe, but I'm willing to find out."

I felt a tear in my eye and said nothing. The E.M.T came out and started preparing for take off.

As he climbed in she looked into my eyes and said, "This is my boyfriend, he has to go."

So it was that a sailor lost on land and an Angel God threw in front of him flew into Gainesville holding hands. So it was that a couple of weeks turned into a couple of years, then into a couple of decades.

KENNESAWTAYLOR

Just Chris Penny

"What's your name son?"

"Just Chris Penny, Sir."

"Dr.. Henderson asked me to stop in and see you. Do you know why?"

"It has something to do with my name, I think."

"What is your name son?"

"Just Chris Penny, Sir. I don't understand the question."

"And what shall we call you Mr. Penny?"

"Just will do fine, Sir."

Dr. Sims paced the small room, rubbing the stubble from a long shift. The smallish room seemed tighter, more cramped than usual. A problem he'd heard over the years from many patients, but one he'd never experienced before. Already sparsely furnished, Mr. Penny had for his part, done nothing to help. On the foot of the bed a pair of jeans and shirt laid, worn but folded neatly, on the floor was a worn pair of penny loafers, pennies included, nothing else to add any depth to this young man at all. No personal effects, no change in his pockets. Just Chris Penny, it was what he kept giving as his name.

"Mr. Penny, will you excuse me just a moment?"

"Sure Sir, I'm not going anywhere it would seem." Just lifted his hands, indicating the room and its locked door.

Dr.. Sims moved to the large white door, leaning in close he looked through the small window laced diagonally with wire inside the glass to make it unbreakable. Dr.. Henderson leaned against the wall on the right side of the door. Eye contact was all that was needed to convey the message. Dr. Henderson rolled around and began placing the key in the door that would allow Dr. Sims out into the hall. Henderson pulled at the overly massive door, Sims moved into the hall as Henderson closed and relocked it. Again, a slight look was all that was need for the two to place their hands in their pockets. The action pushed their lab coats back, giving the appearance of long white tails. They started down the hall at a leisurely pace. From a distance the two middle age doctors would appear to be two carefree students in their first year of residency.

"So what do you think?" Henderson asked.

"He never referred to himself in third person."

"I never said he did, but isn't it the same thing?"

"I don't know, it is odd."

"I've spoken with him for a total of 5 hours and he still says his name is Just, even introduces himself with it."

Sims made an exaggerated move to avoid a nurse moving by in a hurry with purpose. "So what do you know about him?"

"Nothing, he came in with no I.D."

"You've checked in town?"

"Yes, nothing, the sheriff says he'll check the surrounding Counties, see if he can come up with something."

"Okay, I admit something is out of place here."

"Well I guess I shouldn't be so pissed at him, total amnesia is a bitch, all he's got is that damned name. It's aggravating me, must be all the hours."

"Stick with it, maybe we'll find something that'll help."

Just stepped from the barn and closed the door. Stepping back he smoothed his suit and shed the remnants of hay from it. As he turned the Sun shown down on him, confirming what a lovely day it would be, another lovely day in Sandersville Ga. Turning he started across the farm towards a covered bridge that would take him across Lee Creek and to the road that would eventually lead home. The birds sang in the trees around him, not just trees, but apple trees laden with blooms. This was his father's country estate; he'd been coming here all his life. The Spring had been a little dry, puffs of dust rose from his footfalls.

He almost burst into a fit of whistling, but something stopped him. It wasn't a thing, but a small weasel of an idea. Maybe a dark cloud building on the horizon. Looking towards the sky in all directions he saw nothing to indicate an oncoming storm. Crossing the bridge, the sunlight flashed through little gaps in the boards, every ten feet or so there was a window cut from the boards so you could see the creek and to allow light to get in. The boards at his feet made comforting sounds, sounds he'd heard as a child, only now the boards were much older. They squeaked and groaned as his weight fell on them.

When he was a child they had been new, well maybe not new, but only about twenty years old, now they were approaching fifty and had dried, contracted and lost some of their shape and tightness. Stepping off the bridge he turned and ran his fingers along the wood of the bridge face. It was still there. Etched in the wood were the words, Just Chris Penny and Sara Mosley forever. Carved there so long ago; it had taken him a week to do it, a little at a time. Why did his name have to be so long? Again a tinge of impending doom flickered in his mind. First he smiled, but as he removed his hand his face changed to a look of confusion. He studied the dry wood carefully, there above those words was a simple message. The path you walk now has been walked by many, welcome to the journey.

This was new; he'd never seen it before. Studying it more closely it looked like it had been there all along. Turning, he again smoothed his suit and turned to the road towards home. Okay, so maybe it wasn't going to be a crystal clear day, in the distance the sky was a little darker and it was coming from the direction he was headed. A rumble confirmed his suspicions. At least that would account for the strange feeling he'd had a couple of times.

A strange sparkle in the air caught his eye. It was an odd color, he tried to pin it down, but it moved illusively faster than his eye. Here or there a bird's chirp would be a little out of place, too loud or just plain strange sounding. The wind was picking up and thunder was building and coming closer. The sounds of the world were dancing in his mind, but they were being played on a phonograph from his youth, not a modern one. They would warble, drag or crackle a little like one of the wind up record players his mother used to play for him.

Something was wrong with everything; it was becoming more apparent as he moved along. Again that dark feeling crept into his soul. Not too far away now he could see the rain moving across the sky in his direction. Thinking he'd jog a little, he sped up and decided the Walkers Well was a good place to get a drink and wait out the storm. The peaceful windy morning suddenly escalated into a summer storm and he began running to avoid the rain that would be here any moment. When he neared the well shelter, the rain dropped. Only thirty feet more, but he would be soaked.

He swung up onto the platform and clutched at the well drawing heavy breaths from the effort. The storm raged around him, lightening pops moved closer to him making the hair on his neck bristle slightly through his soaked clothing. This storm was making him a little off. Shaking his head he pulled the bucket from the depths and dipped out a large ladle full of water. Drinking deeply he scanned his surroundings; it was then that he saw it, carved into one of the posts holding up the roof. The path you travel is not new; there have been others before you. It looked like it had been there for years, but he'd never seen it before. The ladle made a ringing sound as he dropped it to the floor of the well platform. He moved out into the rain and stood there looking up as the rain pelted him, which did nothing to belay his feelings of doom and gloom.

It had to be the bridge, the well, something was causing this feeling. He'd need to run, move quickly to get away from it. Lightening popped loudly nearby, almost like the sound of a signal gun started him running, once it began there was no stopping. He moved at breakneck speed, his body barely keeping up with his feet. The earth at his feet so dry it made puffs of dust a few moments ago turned to black mud. He fell once, twice and a third time. Every time he scrambled to his feet and fled the cloud that was pursuing him doggedly.

Shadows danced inside the wall of water that limited his sight to about twenty feet. He dared not look around, he dared not slow down. Something was chasing him, maybe whoever had carved those words, maybe more than one of them. The road flattened and straightened, indicating he was crossing

Mr. Peabody's farm. To the right he could see the shadow of his new barn through the fog of water. Abruptly he jerked right and started for it. Dry, yes it would be dry, but it also had a new door that could be locked. Safety at hand, he struggled to negotiate the mud that was a recently plowed field, the corn sprouts beneath his feet were falling over and floating from the deluge. The rain or the direness of his flee made him smash into the barn. Franticly he grabbed at the door until he found the handle. Sliding it open he jumped inside and slammed it shut, then slid the bolt home.

Placing his back to the door he struggled to control his breath. His mind raced. What did the messages mean, where did they come from? By stopping here maybe he'd avoided whatever was after him, maybe he'd tricked them. Suddenly a feeling bubbled up in his head and he jerked around to peer between the cracks in the boards of the door. Nothing was there except for the gray of volumes of rain coming down. He moved about ten feet to his right and found another crack, nothing but a couple of cows in a pen trying desperately to fit under a shelter that was too small for them. Stepping sideways he peered out at every place he could find all the way around the barn, nothing.

What the hell was wrong with him? This was just a storm, he hadn't been afraid of storms since he was a child. Somehow this summer storm had made him into an idiot. He backed across the barn and placed his back against one of the large poles that held up the roof. He slid down into a sitting position with the pole at his back. A thought crossed his mind that he didn't understand. He grasped at it, straining to comprehend it. It slipped away, being far too fast for him to catch.

Near the ceiling of the barn windows were placed under the hip roof to provide some light. A beam of light suddenly burst from the one on the left closest to him illuminating the straw of the barn floor with light. He could hear the rain subsiding, the light started moving through the windows in succession as the sun regained the sky. The barn became fully lighted, the cloud subsided.

A giggle emitted from his mouth, it caught him by surprise. How did a simple storm scare him so badly? It was childish. Standing he ran his hands over his suit again. It was probably ruined, brushing the straw away on his ass, he decided it didn't matter. Running his hands through his hair did wonders to make him feel better. He pushed the water back and down his neck and then shook his hands to dispel most of the water they had collected. Another giggle displaced the last of the dark thoughts brought on by the storm.

Moving across the barn a smile came to his face at the thought of how he'd just ran in here a few moments ago. A little sun was all he needed to chase away the gloom he'd felt. As he approached the door he could just make out the slightest hint of scrawling. The dark feeling excavated at the bottom of his stomach, he fought it. It meant nothing, someone wrote on the door when it was built. Setting his shoulders he moved forward, charging his fear. Placing both hands on the door he slowly looked up, his face just inches from the words carved there. Any Evil in this barn my friend you brought in. That was the thought he couldn't catch, or maybe didn't want to catch.

Deep, deep, deep he could feel it building down deep in his stomach or in his soul. He clenched his teeth tightly to suppress it. He could feel it bubbling, building, and boiling inside. His body felt like the old wood stove at his grandmother's house back in the fifties when he was a small boy. It was radiating almost glowing, but this was building and forcing its way to his mouth. He tilted his head towards the ceiling and out it came. A scream so horrific that it left him drained. He stumbled back and fell, his mind trying to come to grips with a scream that left no doubt of his mental state, put him in a place he never knew, a place he never wanted to go.

He scrambled to his feet and grabbed at the door, slung it open. Mr. Peabody stood not twenty feet away, concern showed on his face yes, but fear too.

"Are you Okay Justin?"

"I'm okay Mr. Peabody, just trying to get out of the rain."

"We heard a scream, was it you?"

I'm fine Sir, I'll talk to you tomorrow."

Justin moved off quickly, head down. There was no way to look Mr. Peabody in the eyes. In fact there was no way to ever look anyone in the eyes again. He was somewhere very few had ever been. Whoever wrote that shit on the walls had been there. Wherever he was going they were pointing the way. Slipping and sliding he trod across the corn field towards the road. Mr. Peabody would not approve, he could have easily moved over and took the driveway, but he didn't have the ability to give a rat's ass. The mud beneath his feet threatened to suck him in if he made the slightest mistake. He had to reach the road, had to run as fast and as far as he could.

Near the road the sodden dirt got worse and his panic became total. He fell and went elbow deep in mud, scrambling frantically he attained the road and struggled to get his feet into the run he needed. As he gained speed large clumps of mud flew through the air, one hitting him in the eye. Running now, but not the way he was going before, instead back the way he'd come. No going home now, no way to get back, he was lost, no way to face his parents. Some part was missing, what was it, who was it? Shaking his hands he tried to fling off all the mud on his arms.

Now there was only to run, never stop, run until he died. As long as he ran he never need talk to anyone about this. The air billowing in and out of his lungs gave him little time for thought; it was a good thing his legs burned. Passing the well he tried to stop so abruptly that he fell on the road. Fighting and clawing his way to his feet he made the platform and grabbed at the bucket of water, still cold from being pulled out of the earth such a short time ago. Pouring it over his head, he turned to look at the words carved on the post. Different words screamed back at him from it. I'll see you when you get there.

The only answer was to run again, run harder, run faster. He jumped back down to the road and ran for his life, for his sanity. Just as his lungs were about to burst the covered bridge materialized out of what was left of his mind. Still slipping he stopped and searched for the words. Just Chris Penny and Sara Mosley forever were there, above it, you're not only on the train, you're the Engineer. Ask Sara, she knows. Glancing towards the barn, he knew that Sara was still there, sleeping in the hay peacefully as he had left her. She would never know what was inside his head now, where he was.

Turning, a sudden bolt of emotions racked his body. He saw Sara dancing, swinging in Mr. Roberts old tire swing, making love in this barn. Stumbling sideways he broke into a run again. The visions of Sara buzzed inside his head like mosquitoes buzz around the outside near the creek in the deep summer nights. There would be no stopping now, he'd run until he died or someone stopped him. Just run as far and fast as he could. How could he ever face anyone again? Not Mr. Peabody, not mother, not father, not Sara.

The room felt warm, the room felt safe, it was well lighted, it was white. Just gripped at the mattress of the bed he sat on with both hands. It felt like it was stuffed with feathers. The air was cool and crisp, but it smelled of stale smoke when the door was opened. The walls were bare with the exception of a map of Milledgeville Ga. on one wall. Standing Just moved to it and studied it carefully. On the bottom right corner was a group of buildings, Central State Hospital it said. Right in the center someone had written in red ink, not only written, but almost carved with red ink. You are here, and they had drawn a star. Good, at least he knew where he was, someone had been looking out for him. He was in the hospital, it was comforting somehow. There were too many questions with no answers.

Dr. Sims stood looking through the small window into Just's room. He heard Dr.. Henderson step up next to him and moved slightly to give him a view. Just Chris Penny stood intently studying the map on his wall. He was young, from a good family probably. One of the many mysteries he'd encountered over the years.

"His name is Justin Christopher Pennington."

Dr. Sims looked at his friend.

"Just Chris Penny, it makes sense now."

"Yes, I guess it does, he's from Sandersville. His dad has money; he's got no record, no history."

"What's he doing here?"

Henderson shook his head. "They found his girlfriend mutilated in a barn two days ago."

"Did he do it?"

Dr. Henderson shrugged his shoulders. "Sheriff says there's no way to tell. I guess that's our job."

"When do we retire again?"

"Twelve years."

Both looked on as Just looked at the map.

"I'll be glad when it's over I hate this fucking job." Sims said.

"Me, too." Henderson mumbled.

Both turned and moved off down the hall in different directions with their coats bunched behind them from their hands being in their pockets. Both tired, both prematurely grey and prematurely old.

The Christmas Rush

All right, even though the Christmas season starts earlier and earlier every year, I continue to be the guy who goes out on Christmas Eve and shops like a madman. Madly rushing from place to place, fighting other idiots who put it off. The traffic is horrible and on this the holiest holiday, the other shopper's attitudes are bad to say the least.

When I was a kid Christmas held much joy, but it held much pain too. In our house we weren't allowed out of our room until our step father came out and he always made sure it was 1:00 PM before he did. Then when you ran to the tree you were overjoyed to see the gifts, but you soon realized how each would get you into trouble in a different way and how they would be taken from you as punishment shortly after the season passed. The bb gun I got in 1969 was taken away and placed on the shelf of my parents closet for a couple of years until some other kid came along that deserved to have it.

This story is about my son and the Christmas of 1984 when he was three. In my house Santa didn't care much for cookies, but he loved chocolate chip cake. So being a real good dad I made sure to make one just for Santa. My son took great joy in cutting a very large piece and placing it with the milk near the tree. Okay, I controlled the piece size. We put him to bed, settled into our chairs in the living room and waited for him to go to sleep to perform our evening duties. I'm ashamed to admit it, but that piece of cake was actually talking to me, giving me come hither looks.

We sat there and waited until we were sure he was asleep and I grabbed Santa's Cake and the milk to perform my first duty of the night, which was to make sure Santa ate the cake. I sliced through the cake with a fork and when it hit the plate it made this sound, tink, it was barely audible. Instantly a blood curdling scream rang from the other end of the house. Daaaaaaaddddyyyyy, it scared the mess out of us. I sat the cake down and we ran to his room. Mom stood in the hall out of sight, while I entered his room to see what nightmare he'd had. He was sitting on the bed furious.

"What happened little buddy?"

"Tell Mommy to quit eating Santa's cake." he said. I heard my wife stifle a laugh in the hallway. I tucked him back in and we had to hustle out on the front porch to laugh in the cold. That he heard the tink was funny enough, but in all the years since we've never figured out why he thought it was his Mom.

Now he was paying attention, but Santa pays attention too. We reentered the house and started assembling some toy or other, we liked to take his stuff out and set it up, not many presents to open. It made for a greater visual when he got to the room in the morning and I, remembering all those Christmases of my childhood, was always there when he woke up. So I was down on the floor doing something, a nasty little surprise peered at me from under the couch. It was a paper grocery bag, back then they didn't ask paper or plastic. It had been stuck in the gas heater at the end of the couch caught on fire then stomped out and shoved under the couch.

It was a scary thought that he had done it when we were in the bed and we were very lucky he didn't set the house on fire. We immediately stuffed it into his stocking in place of the stuff we had bought for it and I went outside and picked a bunch of switches to accompany it. On that Christmas morning there was that look of glee, but there was also a look of horror when he saw the stocking with a letter from Santa to him and one to us about why he'd gotten the switches. I think that was the only time he ever played with fire. It was an easy lesson to teach.

I want to take this time, politically correct or not, to wish all of my readers a Merry Christmas and a Happy New Year. Next week will mark one year of my columns being in the Post and it has been a very good year thanks to all of you. 2010 promises to be a better year with offers coming in from many other states for me to write things. I'll write columns as I travel and I hope you like them.

POETRY, YES POETRY

My First love

She still speaks my name, calling, longing for my return.

Sometimes I still hear her and oh my heart does burn.

Separated by so many miles, so much barren land.

To feel my feet on a deck again to once again be a man.

To taste her salty kiss to hear her winds hiss.

There were years I'd not listen at all

She yearned, mourned and I did not near her call.

As the years slip away from me,

I'm afraid I am what I'll always be,

a man who's still in love with the sea.

So when I'm dead and gone,

Please someone carry me home.

Big Fat Mamma's Pizzaree

Working on a Sunday, is never any fun.

But when you have to do it, you have to get it done.

Sitting at my desk, in early afternoon

I was wishing that the going home would be coming soon.

Nothing ever happens, I never do a thing,

But much to my surprise the phone began to ring.

No one called on Sunday but it continued to sing,

looking down I noticed not the phone, but the fax machine.

Not that strange really, this mistake was often made.

For if you wanted Pizza Hut, our fax is what information gave.

I was really bored, surely this you can see,

so I grabbed the phone and answered Big Fat Mamma's Pizzaree.

The old soul on the other end, had been drinking really bad.

The task that lay before him would take everything he had.

I would like a large pizza he said with onions, peppers and ham.

My name is John, I'm at the inn in town, I think. Yes that's where I am.

Let me read this to you I said so I understand.

You want a pizza with onions, peppers, anchovies and ham.

Anchovies he moaned, what idiot did I call?

Before I'll eat one, I'll eat no pizza at all.

OK, OK, I think I understand.

You want a large pizza onions, peppers, anchovies and ham.

He tried his best, but couldn't make me see,

then he said a lot of words that I can not repeat.

I know that I've been drinking, my voice it isn't clear,
but anchovies I never said, so anchovies you could never hear.
This town is full of idiots he said and you're crazy as a loon.
Then I heard as he threw the phone across the room.
I smiled as I hung up, hating it was done,
but then I hit the redial and the fun had just begun.
He answered in a foul mood, as mad as he could be
I said John, I'm the manager at Big Fat Mamma's Pizzaree.
I just had to fire this guy, he's not wrapped to tight.
I need to check your order, to be sure that it's right.
A large pizza I asked, onions, peppers, anchovies and ham.
No, not anchovies he said, who do you think I am?
Ok, please be patient as you can,
I see you want no anchovies I really understand.
By your voice, I said, I can tell you've had a nip or two.
If it will fix this up, we'll stop at the liquor store for you.
As the manager I want you as happy as can be,
I hope when you're in town again, you call Big Fat Mamma's Pizzaree.
I lay the phone down gently, giggling about it all,
then laughter started everywhere. Everyone in the office had heard the call.
We laughed and talked about poor John for the rest of that the day.
He had helped to pass the time in his little way.
I wonder how long he waited for a pizza that never came.
I figure that he passed out, unsure even of his name.

Tightrope

Sanity is the tightrope beneath my feet.
A thin small thread between me and the street.
The distance to fall isn't that far,
You can never come back to where you are.
Try to tell me you been there too.
Out where the Milky Way is blue.
Try and tell me you regained your mind.
Only to find that it was blind.

I'm Still Lookin

I'm lookin for a place to call home
I'm lookin, but my feet are set on roam
I'm lookin for a place to get some rest
I'm lookin, but I always fail the test
I'm lookin for some friends
I'm lookin, but the lookin never ends
One day I'm gonna settle down
Plant my roots in some small town
I don't know where that town will be
There's still too much I gotta see
I'm lookin, but the lookin never ends
I'm lookin for a place to lay my head
Some place I won't wake up full of dread
I'm waiting for a time to be
Waiting for a time to just be me
Lookin for some friends to call my own
When I turn around, they won't be gone
I guess I just don't understand
What it means for some to be a man
They'll just use you, then they'll set you free
Woooooooooooe is me
I'm still lookin and so alone
Lookin for that place called home

What of You?

My pen was silent way to long,
All the words of my youth long gone.
Never will they pass my lips again,
Gone like leaves in the wind.
Wasted like the days of my youth,
Gone are the words of truth.
Wasted nights, wasted years,
Wasted words, wasted tears.
Life moves on at such a pace,
We move as in a race.
No race to win no finish line,
The race my friend is in our mind.
Can I get it back, can I reclaim,
Or will the race remain the same?
To write I struggle and strive,
Just to live, just to survive.
No education no big deal,
I write from my heart, what I feel.
If you write only from your mind,
You'll write only drivel, every time.
When you write pull it from your soul,
It's the only writing that makes you whole.
The years pass quickly by,
As you go the more you cry.
Waste no more, catch what you can,
All those years never come again.
I will live on for a time,
These years will all be mine.
What of you,
What will you do?
Will you pass leaving no sign,
Leaving only sorrow behind?
I beg you leave something there,
Like words that will linger forever in the air.
What of you,
What will you do?

Why is There War?

Why is there war Daddy
I don't understand
Will I fight a war Dad
When I am a man
Don't ask me these questions son
I asked them too
No one ever answered me
How could I ever answer you
Will I ever go to war Dad
Will I ever fight
Will I kill a young man Dad
Far away in the night
For your innocence son
I can only pray
That in your life
You never see the day
Finally as the tears welled up
In my ten year old's face
He said will I ever die Dad
In some distant place
Don't ask me these questions son
I asked them too
No one ever answered me
How can I ever answer you

If You Fall From the Sky

As a baby I reached for doorknobs, just a little too high.
Bottom smacks the floor, still no open door, I cry.
Eight, I reach for the man I'm to be, but the man comes too late.
I watch Superman beat my mother, jumping in, I'm deciding my own fate.
The falls are harder during that time,
But God has decided that the falls are mine.
Superman gets killed; he too had to fall,
Even though he was reaching down, never reaching up at all.
Fourteen the man had to emerge, nowhere else to run,
I reached for normal, but it has yet to come.
I reached for love, it being the most illusive thing.
I fell often, the pain worse and keen.
I reached for my wife and held her tightly in my grasp.
Finally something real, something that would last.
Reaching still, but the falls are less kind,
For you learn to reach higher every time.
Write a book, fling it out into the world, reach for the sky.
How far is the fall from the sky and if you fall from the sky, will you die?
It's not for me to answer for all others here,
But if I fall from the sky, I'll die with a cheer.

The Boy of No Joy

I'm the boy, the boy of no joy.

I was in your class, a dirty hand, vacant eyes, the soul of a man.

I'm the guy, the guy who'll still cry.

In the darkness the doubt and guilt sits still, waiting on me to return to bid it's will.

I'm the man who walks hand in hand with the boy, the boy of no joy.

I stole your tools, your children's toy.

I'm the boy, who stole my joy?

I'm the kid who you looked at his ribs, look away quick at least he lives.

You and others like you time and again, broken ribs and noses always mend.

I'm the climber, who climbs toward the sky.

If I fall will I die?

I'm the kid you sent to the office time and again.

I had no hope, no future, no friend.

Look away, look away, look away all.

A bad childhood habit, how often I'd fall.

I'm the boy, the boy of no joy.

It was my own little war, a soldier I'd never be.

A prisoner of war was Gods plan for me.

The fist goes up and the fist comes down.

If no one outside hears it, does it really make a sound?

I'm the man who really understands.

The relative size of the head of a child and a hand.

I hope that there is no one anywhere that gets this,

It's my hope, my dream my plea, but I know it's wishful thinking, there are others just like me.

I'm the man with the little boy inside.

The boy still walks the earth, the man's only along for the ride.

Just in case you meet me, I'm the boy, the boy with no joy.

I'm the guy who will cry, the man who has yet to die.

In the end I win, you die, I cry, where do the answers lie?

Die Sweet Child

I've watched men die, held their hand, heard their final breath.

Men who had proved themselves, men who had passed their test.

I've watched men die who needed it, men who had no heart.

I see them in my dreams sometimes, but am glad I did my part.

The words I speak now are so damn true, most will not understand.

Sometimes you wish to die to avoid again, that awful hand.

I hope you can not understand what it means to wish to die.

I understand oh too well and for those kids I cry.

I'm sad each time I hear the news that a child has lost its fight.

But I know in my heart of hearts that they will sleep in peace for the first time that night.

So die sweet child one after one until the world does see.

That they must put a stop to what happened to you and me.

And So We Fight On

And so we fight on,
remembering days long gone.
Starring through the fog and rain,
It's hard not to think of the pain.
Every single day,
Is still a fight in some way.
Every single night,
In sleep we search for the light.
We live, we learn, we love,
but deep down we never really rise above.
We're troubled or trouble and misunderstood,
most of us bad, but some of us are good.
We watch the world around us as normal passes by,
we know not normal, but still we must try.
We wonder why,
why we still must cry.
When young you try to fight all the evil that others
do,
Then you find out, they don't arrest them, they arrest
you.
You go on living watching mothers and children die,
You watch the news each day and in front of
everyone you cry.
Your children do not understand,
to them you'd never raise your voice or hand.
You see them in your church, your school, on the
street,
you see the abuse in the eyes of many children you
meet.
You want to believe it's over, that it's time has past,
but the numbers prove it lives on and that it will last.
So you figure out a way to fight,
a way that society thinks is right.
And you fight on,

you fight on with a poem, a book, a song.
You speak with hail and brimstone as often as you can,
you scream out to the world, abuse me if you can, I am a man.
Others fight the fight as well,
people who never lived the hell.
You hug them, thank them, bless their hearts,
because they are where the end really starts.
And so we fight on,
with an army not alone.
Will we ever stop it, no way.
but we make a difference every day.
We're out there still shivering, scared, trying to survive,
we're counting on all of you to save us and keep us alive.

DON'T LOOK AWAY!

Rip My Soul Free

Informally Educated is a true story of severe child abuse and murder in a small southern town. People ask me all the time how I wrote this book. My sister, who went through this with me, says she could never have done it, says it doesn't even come close to how bad it was. I agree, there are no words in the English language to describe the truth as we know it, as it lives in our hearts until death do us part. We are married to this story. It's funny to us how people read this book and look for things to doubt. We know that if the whole truth were to be written no one would read it. People don't want to really know the whole truth. Right now they can still sleep.

We were denied our education, our childhood, our dreams. On the day Jack Cooper was killed we were set free, allowed to live until adulthood. We thought we were done with all he imposed on us. However, once you experience this kind of trauma as a child, it doesn't go away. In the dark, the stillness, and the quiet the doubt and guilt comes creeping up, whispering in your ear, you are not worthy, you never were, you never will be.

I knew I would write this book on the day a well placed bullet changed our lives forever. First I had to educate myself to do it. It took many years, then I tried to write it out in longhand and had hundreds of false starts. Once I bought my first computer I had the tools and skills.

Tools and skills, you'd think they alone would be all that's needed to write a book, wrong. I sat at my computer for a year and looked into the distance, remembering all those long repressed memories, memories that do not visit but haunt. I cried on my keyboard late into the night as I typed. I relived my childhood that year and it affected every moment of every day. In the end that year healed me in a way that all the years of alcohol and drug abuse were never able to. Writing such a book is similar to ripping out your soul and flinging it onto the paper, it leaves you drained.

When you start, you see the possibility of money. When you write, you see the reward of getting it out. When you publish, you find out that the message is so much more than money. It turns out there are so many of us out there. I get tons of e-mails every day from people who just want to tell their story to someone who understands. Keep them coming, it gives me strength to know you're out there.

<u>kennesawt@gmail.com</u>

I do book signings yes, but they are so much more than that. I meet the people who need to hear this story, the people who know it's true. The people who struggle to pull their souls from a depth that many will never know. Come speak to me, know I understand, help me make a difference in the world.

Misunderstood Heroes

When I was a child I was abused by a control freak, in fact most abusers are control freaks. Therefore, I had many enemies, police officers, preachers, teachers, counselors and any form of social worker that existed at the time. If any of those people had a reason to interrogate me, I sure wasn't saying anything to them and within a week we moved in the middle of the night, losing all friends and everything we had accumulated.

As I grew up I held a certain kind of scorn for those people, because they did nothing to save me. I particularly hated teachers, preachers, and cops. Truth is, many saw what we were going through and turned away or worse, punished us for our dirty hands, disheveled clothing, tendency to fall asleep in class, or just not paying attention. We were concerned with other thoughts, namely the desire to survive another day.

Preachers screamed at us about going to hell while we were forced to slip into the night and steal for our stepfather. Cops came to our house when we fought for our lives and simply left us at the kitchen table bleeding and scared. Many times they never entered the house, but stood in the yard and talked to him, laughing about the latest local sports team or the fishing in the river. There were times that I was taken to the emergency room after the police left.

When I was 14, God used a mobster to pull the trigger and blow that S.O.B's brains out. It was the first night I had a hope of reaching adulthood. I know God had some part in it or they would have executed all of us. Time passed, I fought my demons and think I eventually won. Although late at night, when it's dark and quiet, they still come around to whisper in my ears. I think they always will. It's kind of like Santa. How does he cover the whole world in one night? How does the guilt and fear do it?

I've grown up hearing the horror stories about D.F.A.C.S., foster care and many other organizations all my life and just ignored them. Now, as I try to start to be a child advocate, I've been forced to learn about and understand these agencies and others like C.A.S.A. Here's what I've found out.

As with any system this big, there are bad apples. For every horror story you hear there are thousands of success stories that you never hear about. For every horror story you hear about a bad foster parent, there are thousands of stories of people who have helped up to fifty kids become productive adults and provided them with the love needed to survive and to learn to be loving parents. C.A.S.A. should not even exist, but if they didn't, who would fight for all those kids in court?

Here's the really sad part, we pay spoiled boys millions of dollars to be our heroes just because they can play with balls. Yet our teachers, cops, social workers and others like them live just above the poverty line. They are subjected to the most rotten, foul and ugly situations that they must somehow try to absorb and stay normal and sane.

I've had the opportunity to talk to many in the last few months. This joke kind of sums up what they must endure. What's the difference between a dead dog in the road and a dead D.F.A.C.S. Worker in the road? The dog is the one with the skid marks in front of it.

I've talked to workers who do this job and they have their own horror stories. They can't even admit what they do for a living because people move away from them at parties and even at their own churches they're ignored. This, for a group of people who went into their field to help the innocent of our society and who have become evil somehow for their beliefs. They take their work home because they see so many ugly things every day that the images will not leave them, even in their dreams.

Please realize that these people are not only on the front line of the fight to curb the 9 million cases of child abuse in our Country every year. Not to mention the 5 children who die in America every day at the hands of the people they know, love and trust the most. They are the only people in the damn fight. They are underpaid, overworked and get treated everywhere they go like the enemy. With their numbers and their budget all they can do is keep the figures from growing at a much more alarming rate.

Find someone in one of these agencies today and thank them for being soldiers in what is a war. They do not cause all the abuse problems we have in this Country, they try their best to stop it. We as Americans must stop it. Learn how you can help these real American heroes in their lonely fight.

I salute you for what you try to do and thank each one of you from the bottom of my heart.

Don't Just Break The Cycle, Beat it Over the Head with A Big Baseball Bat

Last week I got an e-mail from Martha Bright, asking me to attend an event at Fort Valley State. Now I've never been to that college or ever heard of Martha Bright. I get many e-mails every week about attending events that have something to do with abuse in some form or fashion. I can hardly attend every one of them. Still some little nagging thing kept picking away at the back of my mind as the week progressed and I kept not deleting her e-mail.

In the end I wrote to her to get directions and planned to make the one and a half hour trip on Friday the 9th of October. I try to spend my meager resources to go where I might have the greater impact or make some kind of connection that will help me make a greater impact on child or spousal abuse. This held no promise to do either, but still that little thing kept nudging me and saying you better be there. The speaker's name didn't jump out at me, but I'd heard of a G.P.B special about her.

Upon arrival I was met by Martha and treated like I was one of her own children. I felt special the moment I arrived, thank you for that you sweet, sweet lady. I was ushered in and had a seat near the front of the auditorium. The moment Johnnetta Mcswain-Clay stood to approach the podium, I knew exactly who she was and remembered watching every second of the special about her. She set about revealing her 12 step program named Breaking the Cycle, Beating the Odds.

She was loud and proud. She spilled her heart out for all to see, but she reached into your heart and threw it to the stage for all to see as well. She was bold and she told things many would never reveal about themselves in public. She was dynamic and the event turned into the equivalent of an old time tent revival with audience members shouting yes, you tell it and Amen throughout. If you were not moved to action, then you have no place in C.A.S.A, the Department of Family and Children's Services, the Peach County Family Connection or any of the other organizations present at the event.

She not only attacked the subject of child and spousal abuse she threw it to the ground and beat it with a bat for all to see. She gave to it the treatment it had given to her for all those horrific years. If you had a doubt about her conviction or purpose, you needed to check your pulse.

She told her story, she told mine, she told the story for all the millions of children and adults out there who have no voice, who can't find their voice. I was very fortunate to give her a copy of my book and spend a good bit of time with her. She was so nice and shared much information and inspiration with me personally. At one point, she asked me my five-year plan. I was dumbstruck. While I had one, I had never had someone ask me what it was. You can bet I e-mailed it to her the next day.

We are such different people, she has a good Education, mine is lacking, but we are the same person, we are siblings in a sick, sick family that neither of us would have chosen. I said to her and I say it again. We will be lifelong friends. I've just got to make her believe it. We will work together all our lives to reach a common goal. Whether we do it together or separated by many miles. Johnnetta now has a part of my heart that I'll never get back and I'm so glad she does.

I want to thank Johnnetta for what she does, how powerful her presentation is and what she has accomplished. She gives hope to so many. I only hope my presentation, Words Have Power, has half the impact that hers does. I salute her, I salute the Peach County Family Connection and its members for arranging and allowing me to be at such an inspirational gathering. Thank you Martha Bright, Frankie Towler and all the other members, I'm sorry I can't remember everyone's names.

My life has changed many times, but it was changed again last Friday by this very special and strong woman. Above all else I want to thank you Johnnetta for that. If you don't know who she is, it's time to find out.

www.breaking-the-cycle.com

EPILOGUE

I guess you noticed that my life has been pretty much dominated by my animals, my cars and all the drinking I did as a young man. I'm afraid that way too much of this book is true. I've had one of the best years of my life and as 2010 kicks off, I've embarked on a journey to criss cross the Country to write a new book named To Look for America.

The other thing that has held much sway on my life was the way I was raised. I've decided to write my way around America and to raise awareness about spousal and child abuse at every opportunity. Thus far people continue to resist the message, still I must continue. The ugly part I can't help and if I change the life of just one person for the better, the broke part will have all been worth it.

I've found that I know who and what I am. It really isn't that bad, once you get used to it.

MORE FROM
KENNESAW TAYLOR

INFORMALLY EDUCATED
THE REDNECK COOKER
THE CRACKER JACK CREW
RAPP 66

WWW.KENNESAWTAYLOR.COM

LaVergne, TN USA
08 August 2010
192555LV00001B/3/P